SHIT GROUND
NO FANS

SHIT GROUND
NO FANS

It's by far the greatest
FOOTBALL SONGBOOK
the world has ever seen

JACK BREMNER

BANTAM PRESS

LONDON · TORONTO · SYDNEY · AUCKLAND · JOHANNESBURG

TRANSWORLD PUBLISHERS
61–63 Uxbridge Road, London W5 5SA
A Random House Group Company
www.rbooks.co.uk

First published in Great Britain
in 2004 by Bantam Press
an imprint of Transworld Publishers.
This revised edition published in 2010.

A CIP catalogue record for this book is available from the British Library.

ISBN 9780593066584

Addresses for Random House Group Ltd companies outside the UK
can be found at: www.randomhouse.co.uk
The Random House Group Ltd Reg. No. 954009

The Random House Group Limited supports the Forest Stewardship
Council (FSC), the leading international forest-certification organization. All our
titles that are printed on Greenpeace-approved FSC-certified paper carry the FSC logo.
Our paper procurement policy can be found at
www.rbooks.co.uk/environment

Designed by www.carrstudio.co.uk
Printed and bound in Great Britain

2 4 6 8 10 9 7 5 3 1

Contents

Introduction

When the original edition of this book appeared in November 2004, I reeled and fell backwards into an uncovered mine-shaft when told that the *Daily Telegraph* had chosen to run a review of it. On coming round, I was less surprised to discover that the man who had gone to the effort of trying to find some lasting merit between its covers was profoundly unimpressed by the fruits of my hard work. Filled with curiosity, I took a final hit of happy gas, discharged myself from the Mister Chuckletrousers Ward and went straight to the hospital shop to buy a copy of the newspaper. Hooting, weeping and bouncing off the walls with laughter, I read the critic's mounting disgust with a disbelief that quickly ballooned into a full-blown fit of foaming hysteria. An orderly eventually arrived and taped off the busy entrance foyer and security operatives were on the scene soon after to cart me off to the funny farm where I have remained ever since. And in the six years that have followed, barely a minute has passed when

my recollection of that review has not triggered another episode of howling and guffawing. The whole experience has definitely affected my relationships with other former Prime Ministers.

In my more lucid moments, usually when watching my banana being mushed up, I often wonder what on earth the reviewer had imagined he was going to read when he ran his finger down the list of sport-related books to be published that week and singled out *Shit Ground No Fans* for his critical scrutiny. He wrote that he had been excited by the prospect of being enlightened about the culture and history of football chants in Britain and, God blind me, was he disappointed! We had hoped, of course, that the title alone would have telegraphed a reasonably strong signal to prospective readers as to the seriousness of the content within. We had even higher hopes that a large box in the corner of the front cover that read 'Warning Adult Content!' might have been the clincher for those still holding their chin, squinting their eyes and wondering whether

Shit Ground No Fans was a) an extremely important academic paper that aims to advance our understanding of British culture and earn its author the Chair of Sociology at Cambridge University or b) a collection of deeply offensive, politically incorrect, morally illiterate, shockingly childish and extremely silly chants from the nation's football grounds. Erm, tricky one.

Alas, we failed. Duped like the critics, tens of thousands of philosophers, professors and other sensitive literary types ordered copies of the book, only to choke on their pipes on opening it up to discover hundreds of repulsive songs about sheep-shagging rustics, thieving Scousers, obese Geordies, criminal Cockneys, ginger pubic hair and inbred families from Burnley. The legal actions wear on. One poor chap actually swallowed his corncob pipe and died. He had gone straight to the Millwall section.

So, by way of disclaimer, let's make it perfectly clear from the outset of this updated edition that *Shit Ground No Fans* is NOT a serious academic paper. It is a very silly book. We should also like it to be known that many of the statements contained within it are based on the indisputable truth that: all girls from Glasgow wear moustaches, men from Cardiff prefer livestock to women, all Continental types are hairy and smelly, Britain has won two World Wars to Germany's none, all Ipswich males are rapists, everyone in Gillingham lives in a caravan, you have to be overweight, blind and illegitimate to get a job as a referee, every brother living in the North West is married to his sister, Merseyside is an open prison and all the men in Grimsby sleep with sea bass. And anyone who didn't already know that is a granny-shagging junkie village imbecile.

At the risk of upsetting the Fun Police still further, I have to tell you that this latest edition is considerably more offensive and amusing than the original. While the atmosphere inside some grounds may not be what it was before the introduction of all-seater stadiums, I like to think that this collection of filth represents an eloquent rebuttal to the argument that British terrace culture has been dying. If anything, the quality of the wit, the inventiveness, the spontaneity, the prejudice, the silliness, the vulgarity and the brutal vindictiveness of the average British football chant just gets better and better.

Author's Note:

There are over four hundred new chants here, replacing the least funny, inventive, cruel and relevant ones from the original. (I have retained all the classics and the best of the rest.) As before, the only criterion for a chant to get in the book is that it is funny. Millions of chants are sung at British grounds every year. Each week dozens, even hundreds, of new ones or variations on old themes are sung from Inverness to Plymouth, Swansea to Norwich. A man could spend several lives tracking down every single amusing chant that has been sung around the country over a six-year period. The only apology therefore that I'd like to make is to the fans who feel that the humour of their club has not been properly represented. With the exception of Walsall fans, of course, most readers will be intelligent enough to understand that for reasons of space and avoiding repetition, not every funny chant sung at every club can be included. Everyone else can sod off back to their slums, be they northern or southern.

Professor Jack Bremner, 2010

Clubs A–Z

VIP
GUESTS

Welcome to Shielfield Park

HOME TO

BERWICK RANGERS FC

CARAVAN HOLIDAY HOMES FOR SALE
TEL: BERWICK (01289) 381333
E - MAIL www.british-holidays.co.uk

Clubs A-Z

Aberdeen

Shall we poach? (x2)

Shall we poach an egg for you?

Aberdeen supporters to Rangers' Kirk Broadfoot, who was hospitalized when the egg he was microwaving exploded in his face.

♪: *'Bread Of Heaven'*

The girls all have moustaches

They've all got nasty rashes

And nae c**t ever washes

You're the Dundee Family

♪: *'Addams Family'*

The wrong f***ing country

You're in the wrong f***ing country

The wrong f***ing country

Sung to Rangers and Celtic fans.

♪: *'Guantanamera'*

We're red, you're dead
We're bouncing on your head
Aberdeen, Aberdeen

No soap in Glasgow
There's no soap in Glasgow (x10)

♪: 'Guantanamera'

Northern Ireland is shit (x10)

Sung to Rangers and Celtic fans

♪: 'We Love You, We Do'

Arsenal

One man went to laugh
Went to laugh at Tottenham
One man and his dog
Went to laugh at Tottenham

Two men went to laugh etc

Alex Hleb, Alex Hleb
Running down the wing
Alex Hleb, Alex Hleb
In a big white van
He comes from Belarus
Sells cheap fags and booze
Alex Hleb, Alex Hleb, Alex Hleb

Welcoming their new midfielder from the Baltic state.

𝄞: *'Robin Hood, Riding Through The Glen'*

Osama wo-ah-oh (x2)

He supports the Ar-se-nal!

He's hiding near Kabul!

Osama wo-ah-oh (x2)

He's in the Taliban!

He is an Arsenal fan!

After newspaper reports that Bin Laden supported Arsenal as a young man.

𝄞: *'Volare'*

One Song!

We've only got one Song

Arsenal fans about midfielder Alex Song.

Celtic fans: Shall we sing a song for you?

Arsenal fans: Shall we score a goal for you?

During a Champions League game.

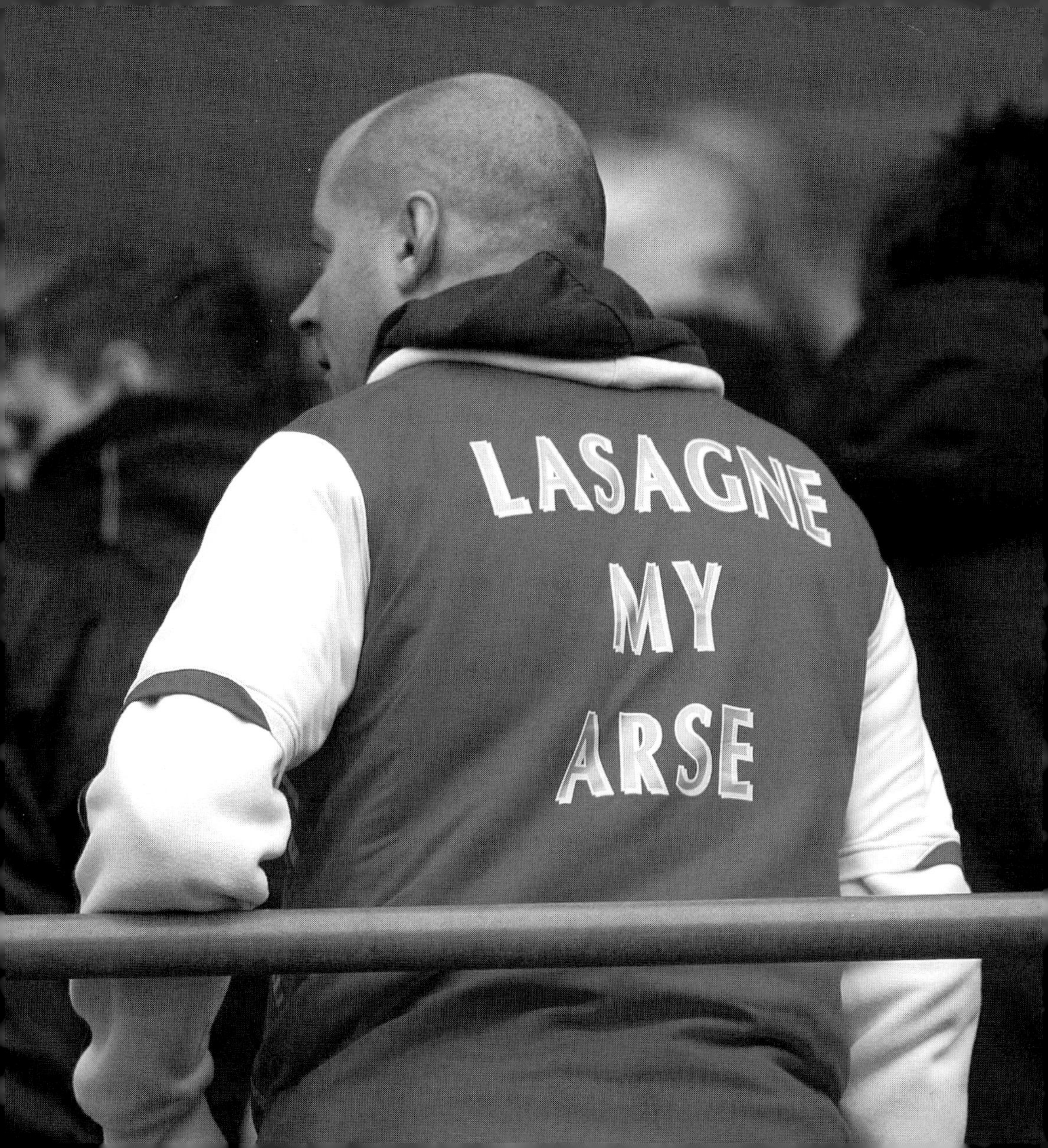
LASAGNE
MY
ARSE

He's five foot four (x2)
We've got Arshavin
F**k Adebayor!

Hailing the diminutive Russian.

He's small, he's shit
He's in a child's kit
Arshavin! Arshavin!

Tottenham fans take a different view.

Green in a minute
He's going green in a minute!

When Porto's Hulk touched the ball in a
Champions League game.

♪: 'Guantanamera'

Diaby, wo-ah-oh (x2)
He comes from Gay Pa-ree
He knocked out John Terry

♪: 'Volare'

Sing when you're drawing
You only sing when you're drawing

Arsenal fans to PSV in obscure reference to Dutch masters.

There's only one Theo Walcott, one Theo Walcott
With his lightning pace and baby face
Walking in a Walcott Wonderland!

For he's a jolly good Vela (x2)
For he's a jolly good Velaaaa!
Which nobody can deny

Tribute to Mexican striker Carlos Vela.

We'll race you back to London!

Arsenal fans at Old Trafford.

Eduardo, wo-ah-oh (x2)
He's got no football skills, he walks like Heather Mills

Taunting of sidelined Arsenal striker about his hideous leg fracture.

𝄞: 'Volare'

Aston Villa

Sunday, Monday, Habib Beye!
Tuesday, Wednesday, Habib Beye!
Thursday, Friday, Habib Beye!
Saturday, Habib Beye!

Aston Villa fans take up the former Newcastle tribute to their defender.

🎼: 'Happy Days'

You're Chelsea's feeder club! (over and over)

Sung to West Ham.

🎼: Verdi's 'La Donna E Mobile'

We'll meet again
Don't know where
Don't know when
But I know we'll meet again some sunny day!

Sung to teams facing relegation, or lower league sides in the cup.

🎼: Vera Lynn's 'We'll Meet Again'

Sit down, potato head (over and over)

Sung to Steve Bruce when he was manager of Birmingham City.

𝄞: *'La Donna E Mobile'*

Nice one, Shearer
Job well done
Nice one, Shearer
Now back to Channel One

Congratulating the BBC pundit on
taking Newcastle down.

Barnsley

New ground, new fans

At Hull's shiny new KC Stadium.

♪: *'Big Ben Chimes'*

Fishing till you die

You'll be fishing till you die
You know you are
You're sure you are
You'll be fishing till you die

Sung to Hull and Grimsby.

Bra-zil

It's just like watching Bra-zil

♪: *'Blue Moon'*

Birmingham City

One man went to rape
Went to rape Lee Bowyer
One man and his cellmate
Went to rape Lee Bowyer

Two men went to rape etc

Sung to Lee Bowyer throughout his career at various clubs whenever he appears in court, is fined or charged, etc. Not sung by Birmingham fans, of course ...

Fahey's a jolly good fellow (x3)
And so say all the rest

Birmingham fans honour Irish midfielder Keith Fahey.

Don't cry for me, Aston Villa

The truth is I cannot stand you

All through my wild days

My mad existence

We took the Holte End

Without resistance

🎼: *'Don't Cry For Me Argentina'*

Sing when you're robbing

You only sing when you're robbing

A traditional Birmingham welcome for Liverpool and Everton fans, often followed by ...

🎼: *'Guantanamera'*

He-e-e-ey Scousers

Ooh! Ah!

I want to kno-o-o-ow

Where's my vide-o?

🎼: *'Hey Baby'*

We are Brummies, we are Brummies

We are Brummies, yes we are

You are wankers, you are wankers

You are wankers, yes you are

♪: *'Sailing'*

You can stick your Jasper Carrott up your arse (x2)

You can stick your Jasper Carrott

Stick your Jasper Carrott

Stick your Jasper Carrott up your arse

Opposition fans greet Birmingham's celebrity supporter.

♪: *'She'll Be Coming Round The Mountain'*

Blackburn Rovers

Hands up, baby, hands up
Show me your six fingers! (x2)

To Burnley.
𝄞: Ottawan's 'Hands Up'

He drinks! He drives!
He spits in people's eyes!
El-Hadji Diouf, El-Hadji Diouf!

Celebrating the striker's brushes with the law.

You better watch out, you better beware
He's good on the ground and he's good in the air
Santa Cruz is coming to town

Blackburn fans at Christmas time, before Santa took his gifts to Man City.

In the town where I was born

Lived a man who sailed to sea

And he told me of a tale

Of a town called Burnley

Burnley fans eat ...

... Bananas with their feet, bananas with their feet,

bananas with their feet

🎵: *'Yellow Submarine'*

Blackpool

Your mum's your dad

Your dad's your mum

You're interbred

You're Burnley scum

🎵: *The Piranhas' 'Tom Hark'*

Away in a manger

No crib for a bed

The little Lord Jesus looked up and he said:

F**k off, Preston!

F**k off, Preston!

Burnley have also been known to receive a rendition of this Christmas favourite.

Do you work? (x2)

Do you work in B&Q?

Visiting fans ridicule the tangerine strip.

♪: 'Bread Of Heaven'

Are you stewards? (x2)

Are you stewards in disguise?

Swansea fans pick up the tangerine theme.

♪: 'Bread Of Heaven'

Come on a donkey

You must have come on a donkey

Blackpool fans are often treated to this one when only a few have been able to make it to an away ground.

♪: 'Guantanamera'

Bolton Wanderers

Ginger Mourinho (*ad nauseam*)

Bolton laud rusty-haired gaffer Gary Megson (for a while, at least).

🎼: *'La Donna E Mobile'*

He tackles and he passes
He wrestles and harasses
He gets up people's arses
He's better than Zidane
Gavin McCann! Gavin McCann!

🎼: *'Addams Family'*

Who's the midget? (x2)
Who's the midget in the suit?

Opposition fans to another former Bolton manager, Sammy Lee.

🎼: *'Bread Of Heaven'*

You put your transfer in, your transfer out

In out, in out, you f**k your club about

You do the Cristiano and you change your mind

That's what it's all about ...

Oh, Ronaldo is a wanker!

𝄞: *'Hokey Cokey'*

Bournemouth

Bournemouth have never forgiven Leeds for a drunken rampage through the town on a hot Bank Holiday in 1990 and they have been enjoying the Yorkshire club's spectacular fall from grace:

Champions League to the LDV (all match)

𝄞: *'Tom Hark'*

You all live in a cardboard box

𝄞: *'Yellow Submarine'*

We pay your benefits

𝄞: *'La Donna E Mobile'*

If you follow Leeds United then you must be f***ing scum

(More of a shout than a tune.)

We all love our grannies and our grandads too
We all love our grannies, come on, don't you?
All together now

Paying respect to the town's large retirement community.

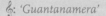 *'Over Land And Sea'*

Bradford City

One Peter Ridsdale
There's only one Peter
Ridsdale

Taunting Leeds over their demise under former
big-spending chairman Peter Ridsdale.

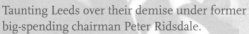 *'Guantanamera'*

Brentford

Build a bonfire, build a bonfire
Put the Fulham on the top
Queens Park Rangers in the middle
And let's torch the f***ing lot

'Oh My Darling Clementine'

Super, super Mark
Super, super Mark
Super, super Mark
Supermarket trolley!

Baffling the opposition.

Brighton & Hove Albion

A cat! A cat!

A cat! A cat! A cat!

Brighton fans play on old 'Attack!' chanted when a cat appears on the pitch.

Brighton fans have long had to endure the somewhat dated and politically incorrect jibes by rival fans about the city's large gay community. Here are some of the more printable taunts:

Down with your boyfriend

You're going down with your boyfriend

♪: *'Guantanamera'*

Does your boyfriend? (x2)

Does your boyfriend know you're here?

♪: *'Bread Of Heaven'*

We can see you (x2)

We can see you holding hands!

♪: *'Bread Of Heaven'*

Stand up cos you can't sit down (over and over)

 'Go West'

You're too ugly (x2)
You're too ugly to be gay

Home fans' response.

 'Bread Of Heaven'

You only work in the summer
Work in the summer
You only work in the summer

Opposition fans take issue with locals over their seasonal employment patterns.

 'Guantanamera'

Down with the pier
You're going down with the pier

Referring to the fire that destroyed one of the city's landmarks.

 'Guantanamera'

I know a fat old policeman

He's always on the beat

That fat and jolly red-faced man

He really is a treat

You'll always find him laughing

He's never known to frown

The reason for his jollity

Is that Brighton's going down

Only known to be sung by Crystal Palace fans, who have a special contempt for Brighton. Don't ask ...

♪: *'The Laughing Policeman'*

Bristol City

He's red, he's white

He thinks the gas are shite

Santa Claus! Santa Claus!

Bristol City to the 'gasheads' of local rivals Rovers over Christmas.

When the City are playing frightful
We've got our Dutchman so delightful
And even though he's just on loan
Evander Sno, Evander Sno, Evander Sno!

Welcoming on-loan Ajax midfielder.
𝄞: *'Let It Snow'*

City, wherever you may be
We went down from One to Three
We'll be back through to win all three
We'll go down in history

𝄞: *'Lord Of The Dance'*

They should have built a wall not a bridge (x2)
They should have built a wall
Should have built a wall
They should have built a wall not a bridge

Sung to Cardiff and Swansea fans.
𝄞: *'She'll Be Coming Round The Mountain'*

You can stick your f***ing dragon up your arse (x2)

You can stick your f***ing dragon

Stick your f***ing dragon

You can stick your f***ing dragon up your arse

𝄞: *'She'll Be Coming Round The Mountain'*

Bristol Rovers

Inbreds and roundabouts

Sung to Swindon.

𝄞: *'La Donna E Mobile'*

Always shit on the Welsh side of the bridge
La la la, la la la, la la la

A favourite of both Bristol teams.

𝄞: *'Always Look On The Bright Side Of Life'*

He's only a poor little Robin

His wings are all tattered and torn

He made me feel sick

So I hit him with a brick

And now he don't sing any more

♪: 'He's Only A Poor Little Sparrow'

If I had the wings of a sparrow

If I had the arse of a crow

I'd fly over City tomorrow

And shit on the bastards below

Shit on, shit on, shit on the bastards below, below

Shit on, shit on, I'd shit on the bastards below

Another old classic for neighbours the Robins, to the tune of 'My Bonnie Lies Over The Ocean'.

Burnley

We fetched him from Scotland and gave him a job
He f***ed off to Bolton cos he's a knob
We asked him to stay
He answered us nay
Saying budgets like yours I can spend in a day
And it's Judas Coyle
We don't love you no more
We hate you, Judas
You money-loving whore

Burnley get emotional after manager Owen Coyle took a job at local rivals.

You can shove your f***ing tower up your arse (x2)
You can shove your f***ing tower
Shove your f***ing tower
You can shove your f***ing tower up your arse

Sung to Blackpool fans.

𝄞: 'She'll Be Coming Round The Mountain'

Their mums go out and sell themselves

For cash, for cash

Their sisters have a handlebar

Moustache, moustache

Their fans are ugly and they're dumb

They bang and bang that f***ing drum

They're bastard Rovers

Knuckle-dragging scum

Sung to Blackburn.

♪: 'When Johnny Comes Marching Home'

He's sewing bags

He's sewing bags

Oyston's sewing bags

A heartfelt tribute to Blackpool chairman Owen Oyston after he was jailed for raping a 16-year-old model.

♪: 'Three Lions'

Chairman Jackie Walker went up to the pearly gates (x3)

And this is what St Peter said:

Who the f**k are Bastard Rovers? (x3)

The Clarets go marching on! On! On!

One for the former chairman of bitter rivals Blackburn.

♪: *'Mine Eyes Have Seen The Glory'*

Your father had your mother

Your sister and your brother

You all sleep with one another

You're the Burnley Family

Your town is twinned with Hell

You're ugly and you smell

This ought to ring a bell

You're the Burnley Family

♪: *'Addams Family'*

Town full of Nazis
You're just a town full of Nazis

Visitors to Burnley, following a successful local election for the far-right BNP.

🎼: *'Guantanamera'*

Always look on the Turf Moor for shite

More lip from visitors to the hallowed ground.

Cardiff City

Robbie Fowler's magic

He's got a cracking shot

And when he signed for Cardiff

He said 'I'm buying Splott'

He bought up half the Valleys and all the Gurnos too

And forty thousand Bluebirds said

'We're gonna live with you!'

Cardiff welcome the Liverpool property magnate to Wales.

𝄞: *'My Old Man's A Dustman'*

God made rivers

God made lakes

God made Swansea

But we all make mistakes

The Bluebirds get biblical.

When the boss says he'll stay
Then he's gone the next day
That's Roberto

He was a Swansea fanatic
But now he's a Latic
That's Roberto

One call on his phone
And now he's gone back home
That's Roberto

They said please don't leave
Then he went and replaced Steve
That's Roberto

They thought he was white
But that changed overnight
That's Roberto

He's not coming back

So f**k off all you jacks

That's Roberto

Cardiff enjoy sudden departure of Swansea boss Roberto Martinez to Wigan.

🎼: *'That's Amore'*

Lee Trundle is a fat t**t

He wears a fat t**t's hat

And when he sees a big fat pie,

he says, 'I fancy that!'

He eats it in his left hand, he eats it in his right

And when he sees a Burger King, he stays all f***ing night

Having a go at the Swansea striker's diet.

🎼: *'My Old Man's A Dustman'*

Always shit on the English side of the bridge

🎼: *'Always Look On The Bright Side Of Life'*

I can't read

And I can't write

But that don't really matter

Cos I is a Bristol City *(or Rovers)* fan

And I can drive my tractor

Steer to the left

Steer to the right

It don't really matter

Cos when it comes to shagging my wife

I'd rather 'ave me tractor

Also ...

You're going home on a combine harvester ...

Fat Eddie Murphy

You're just a fat Eddie Murphy

Opposition fans to Jimmy Floyd Hasselbaink

♪: *'Guantanamera'*

You wish you were Ing-er-lish (over and over)

Sung by opposition fans.

♪: *'La Donna E Mobile'*

You can stick your f***ing rugby up your arse (x2)
You can stick your f***ing rugby
Stick your f***ing rugby
You can stick your f***ing rugby up your arse

One for the muddied oafs at the Millennium Stadium and the Arms Park.

♪: *'She'll Be Coming Round The Mountain'*

One–nil to the sheep-shaggers ...

♪: *'Go West'*

You like shagging sheep (x2)
You like shagging (x2)
You like shagging sheep

♪: *'Knees Up Mother Brown'*

And ...

I'd rather shag a woman than a sheep (x2)
I'd rather shag a woman
Rather shag a woman
I'd rather shag a woman than a sheep – sideways!

𝄞: *'She'll Be Coming Round The Mountain'*

And ...

What's it like to? (x2)
What's it like to ram a lamb?

𝄞: *'Bread Of Heaven'*

There's definitely a theme emerging here ...

Oi! Cardiff!
Leave them sheep alone

𝄞: *Pink Floyd's 'Another Brick In The Wall'*

Carlisle United

We'd rather shag a sheep than a lass (x2)

We'd rather shag a sheep

Rather shag a sheep

We'd rather shag a sheep than a lass

Bristolians and the Welsh are not the only fans with sheep issues.

: 'She'll Be Coming Round The Mountain'

Cumbria, my Lord, Cumbria

Cumbria, my Lord, Cumbria

Cumbria, my Lord, Cumbria

O Lord, Cumbria

: 'Kumbaya'

A small town in Scotland

You're just a small town in Scotland

Sung by opposition fans.

: 'Guantanamera'

Celtic

Rule Britannia, building society
Rangers will never, ever, ever be debt free

Havin' a party when Thatcher dies (x2)
There'll be jelly and ice cream when Thatcher dies
Jelly and ice cream when Thatcher dies

Let's all go to the Pound Shop
Where Rangers buy their home top
La la la, la la la!

He's fast
He's green
He hates the f***ing queen
Robbie Keane, Robbie Keane!

Huns without the bus fare

Youz are Huns without the bus fare!

Sung to Hearts fans. (NB For English fans, 'Huns' are Rangers. Don't get involved. It's to do with the monarchy, House of Hanover, etc.)

&: *'Guantanamera'*

They'll be jumping out of windows when we win (x2)

They'll be jumping out of windows

Jumping out of windows

They'll be jumping out of windows when we win

Well I hope it's multi-storey when you jump (x2)

Well I hope it's multi-storey

Hope it's multi-storey

Well I hope it's multi-storey when you jump

Well I hope it's spiky railings when you land (x2)

Well I hope it's spiky railings

Hope it's spiky railings

Well I hope it's spiky railings when you land

Well I hope it's Catholic doctors when you die (x2)
Well I hope it's Catholic doctors
Hope it's Catholic doctors
Well I hope it's Catholic doctors when you die

One of those lovely sectarian ones only Glasgow can produce.

𝄞 *'She'll Be Coming Round The Mountain'*

Said Lizzie to Philip as they sat down to dine
I've just had a note from an old friend of mine
His name is 'Big Geordie', he's loyal and true
And his dirty big nose is a light shade of blue

He says that the Rangers are right on their game
And ask for a trophy to add to their fame
I'll send up a cup that the Rangers can win
Said Philip to Liz, Watch the Celts don't step in

Said Lizzie to Philip, They don't stand a chance
I'll send up my Gunners to lead them a dance
With Celtic defeated the way will be clear
A cup for the Rangers in my crowning year

But alas for their hopes for the loyal true blues
The Celts beat the Gunners and Manchester too
Beat Hibs in the final and oh what a scene
Sure Hampden was covered in banners of green

Said Lizzie to Philip when she heard the grim news
A blow has been struck at our loyal true blues
Oh tell me, dear Philip, and you ought to know
How to keep Glasgow Celtic defeated below

Said Philip to Lizzie, There's only one way
I've known of their secret for many a day
To keep the Celts down you will have to deport
All the mad fighting Irish that gives them support

Known as the Coronation Cup chant.

Charlton Athletic

Zheng Zhi, wherever you may be
You sell dodgy DVDs
Could've been worse
Could've been Millwall
Selling crack in a primary school

Hailing their Chinese defender.
𝄞: *'Lord Of The Dance'*

Oh, Andy Hunt (x2)
Oh, Andy Hunt, he plays up front
He's got a name like a fanny
Oh, Andy Hunt, he plays up front

𝄞: *'When The Saints Go Marching In'*

Let's all laugh at Palace (x2)
La la la, la la la

To the same tune as 'Let's All Have A Disco'/'Let's All Do The Conga'/'Let's Go F***ing Mental' etc.

Chelsea

Does the dentist? (x2)
Does the dentist know you're here?

Chelsea to the dentally handicapped Ronaldinho.

🎼: *'Bread Of Heaven'*

You're supposed (x2)
You're supposed to be in jail!

Chelsea to Liverpool's Steven Gerrard after his fracas with a DJ.

🎼: *'Bread Of Heaven'*

Who let the Drogs out
Who, who, who, who!

Speak f***ing English
Why don't you speak f***ing English?

To Newcastle, Sunderland and Middlesborough.

🎼: *'Guantanamera'*

Bosingwa in the rain (x2)

What a glorious feeeeeeling

We've gone top again!

Tribute to full-back Jose Bosingwa as the heavens opened.

𝄞: *'Singing In The Rain'*

Abramovich, Abramovich, buying all the men

Abramovich, Abramovich, showing off to Ken

Steals from the poor

Gives to the rich

Abramovich, Abramovich, Abramovich

Chelsea salute their Russian owner with a little dig at former owner Ken Bates.

𝄞: *'Robin Hood, Riding Through The Glen'*

Home in five minutes!

You'll be home in five minutes!

To Man United fans at Stamford Bridge.

𝄞: *'Guantanamera'*

Chelsea, wherever you may be
Don't leave your wife with John Terry
Cos he likes a shag
He likes his fluff
And he'll get your missus up the duff!

Chelsea, wherever you may be
Don't leave your wife with John Terry
It could be worse
He could be Scouse
He'd f**k your wife then rob your house

The opposition revels in the extra-curricular activities of the Chelsea skipper.
𝄞: 'Lord Of The Dance'

Father of the year? You're having a laugh
(over and over)

Debt-free wherever you may be
We're going to buy everyone we see
And we don't give a f**k
About the transfer fee
Cos we are the wealthy CFC!

&: *'Lord Of The Dance'*

Does your butler? (x2)
Does your butler know you're here?

Opposition to posh home fans (also sung at Fulham).

&: *'Bread Of Heaven'*

Following newspaper stories about lurid pictures being sent from Ashley Cole's phone, the songs tumbled from the terraces. Below is just a selection ...

Ashley Cole wears big Ys
He got caught out telling lies
Cheryl won't have him as a sub
So he's off to join a singles club

Knick knack paddy whack
Give the dog a bone
Don't lend Ashley's mate your phone

Ashley Cole, you're on your own
Cos you sent photos from your phone
Laying there, hard and proud
Now you've lost your Girl Aloud

Is that all? (x2)
Is that all she gets at home?

To a male streaker.

𝄞: 'Bread Of Heaven'

You're Shish and you know you are
You're Shish and you know you are

Chelsea to the fans of Turkish club Galatasaray at Stamford Bridge.

𝄞: 'Go West'

Oh the KGB are knocking on his door

Cos he stole all his money from the poor

When the Kremlin get his number

Chelsea's goin' under

Oh the KGB are knocking on his door

Man United fans taunt Chelsea's Russian owner, Roman Abramovich, during the 2008 Champions League final in Moscow.

♪: *'She'll Be Coming Round The Mountain'*

Ten men couldn't lift

Couldn't lift Frank Lampard

Ten men and their forklift truck

Couldn't lift Frank Lampard!

Nine men went to lift etc

Opposition fans taunt Chelsea and England midfielder 'Fat' Frank Lampard.

♪: *'One Man Went To Mow'*

Cheltenham Town

Gone to the races

You should have gone to the races

To losing visitors, especially around the time of the Festival.

♪: *'Guantanamera'*

They go down the cellar for something to eat

They find a dead body and think it's a treat

In their Gloucester slums!

Inspired by serial killer Fred West, a native of Gloucester.

Chesterfield

You can shove your crooked spire up your arse (x2)

You can shove your crooked spire

Shove your crooked spire

You can shove your crooked spire up your arse!

Sung by opposition fans, generally Mansfield.

♪: *'She'll Be Coming Round The Mountain'*

Town full of nobheads
You're just a town full of nobheads!

Sung to local rivals Mansfield.

: *'Guantanamera'*

Colchester United

We can't see you (x2)
We can't see you sneaking out!

To Southampton fans when thick fog descended at the WHC stadium.

: *'Bread Of Heaven'*

Stayed in a burger!
You should have stayed in a burger!

And ...

Shit in the burger!
You're just the shit in the burger!

Opposition fans to United's Dean Gerken.

: *'Guantanamera'*

Coventry City

Oh I do like to be beside the seaside

Oh I do like to be beside the sea

Oh I do like to walk along the prom, prom, prom

Where the brass bands play

F**k off West Brom and Birmingham

F**k off West Brom and Birmingham

We speak with an accent exceedingly rare

You want a cathedral, we've got one to spare

In our Coventry homes

In our Coventry homes

𝄞: *'In My Liverpool Home'*

Crewe Alexandra

Only two Gary Roberts
There's only two Gary Roberts

Sung in 2008 when Crewe had two players of that name.

🎼: *'Guantanamera'*

Crystal Palace

Millwall, you are Millwall
No one hates you, no one cares

Winding up Millwall.

🎼: *'Sailing'*

You fill up my senses
Like a gallon of Fosters
Like a packet of Bensons
Like a line of cocaine
A day's racing at Lingfield
A night out at Sinatra's
For you are my Palace
Come fill me again ...

🎼: *John Denver's 'Annie's Song'*

Away in a manger
No crib for a bed
The little Lord Jesus sat up and he said
We hate Millwall and we hate Millwall
We are the Millwall haters!

We scored five

They scored none

Brighton take it up the bum

With a knick knack paddy whack

Give a dog a bone

Why don't Brighton f**k off home

All in all you're just a bunch of pricks from Millwall!

♪: *'Another Brick In The Wall' by Pink Floyd*

Dagenham & Redbridge

Pub team from Essex

We're just a pub team from Essex

Taunting so-called bigger clubs.

♪: *'Guantanamera'*

Derby County

Wise, Wise, whatever have you done
You've put Leeds in Division One
You won't win a cup
You won't win a shield
Your biggest game will be Huddersfield

♪: 'Lord Of The Dance'

His name is Billy Davies
He's short and rather fat
He said that Clough assaulted him
The vile little t**t
The stupid f***ing red dog
Really is a c**k
Now f**k off back to Scotland
You sweaty f***ing jock

Crikey. Whatever could the ex-Derby Forest manager have done?

♪: 'My Old Man's A Dustman'

Could be worse,
We could be Leeds (repeat *ad nauseam*)

Reassuring the home fans.

𝄞: *'Tom Hark'*

Sing when you're shearing
You only sing when you're shearing!

Sung by opposition fans.

𝄞: *'Guantanamera'*

Doncaster Rovers

Drink, drink, wherever we may be
We are the drunk and disorderly
And we will drink wherever we may be
For we are the drunk and disorderly

𝄞: *'Lord Of The Dance'*

I am a Donny fan
I am a Yorkshire man
If there is one thing that I do
I'll destroy the Rotherham!

Dundee

Davie Dodds
The elephant man
Davie Dodds
The elephant man

An old classic for the facially challenged former Dundee United striker.

𝄞: 'Tom Hark'

You are a weegie

A smelly weegie

You're only happy on giro day

Your mum's out stealing

Your dad's a dealer

Please don't take my hubcaps away

In case any English are wondering, a 'weegie' is a GlasWEGian.

 'You Are My Sunshine'

One shoe!

You've only got one shoe!

To impoverished visitors from Glasgow, etc.

 'Blue Moon'

Let's all laugh at United

Ha ha ha, ha ha ha, ha ha ha

Dundee United

Ginger pubes are unacceptable (*ad nauseam*)

To redheaded opposition players/managers/stewards/police/physios.

𝄞: *'You're So Shit It's Unbelievable'*

Nipples! Nipples!
We want nipples!

To female stewards and half-time dancers.

𝄞: *more grunt than tune*

Sit down, shoot up (*ad nauseam*)

To Glasgow and Edinburgh teams.

𝄞: *'Big Ben Chimes'*

Dunfermline

Shouldn't you? (x2)

Shouldn't you be selling drugs?

To Glasgow and Edinburgh teams.

♪: 'Bread Of Heaven'

Everton

Davie Moyes! Davie Moyes!
He's got red hair
But we don't care
Davie, Davie Moyes

Davie Moyes! Davie Moyes!
He's got red pubes
But we don't lose
Davie, Davie Moyes

Everton fans reassure the manager about the colour of his hair.

🎼: *'Hooray! Hooray It's A Holi-holiday'*

When your club record buy
Grows his hair three feet high
That's … Fellaini

Admiring the Belgian's massive Afro.

🎼: *'That's Amore'*

Tim Timminy

Tim Timminy

Tim Tim Teroo

We've got Tim Howard and he says, 'F**k you!'

Everton fans show their affection for their American goalkeeper Tim Howard, who suffers from Tourette's Syndrome, a neurological disorder that causes nervous tics and uncontrolled verbal outbursts.

Everton fans: You're supposed to be at home

Home fans: You're supposed to burgle homes

He's quick

He's game

We can't pronounce his name

Russian lad! Russian lad!

Home fans welcome Russian midfielder Diniyar Bilyaletdinov.

Leave the alloys (x2)

Leave the alloys on my car

𝄞: *'Bread Of Heaven'*

Who's that fat lad they call Rooney?
He's the kid who's not so bright
Oh we loved you, that's for sure
'Til you went and joined Man-ure
Now we hate your guts, you fat-arsed little shite

And ...

He's fat
He's round
He'll shag your gran for forty pound
Wayne Rooney! Wayne Rooney!

Leighton Baines
I bet you think this song is about you

To their full-back.

♪: Carly Simon's 'You're So Vain'

City of Culture?
You're havin' a laugh (repeat till bored)

♪: 'Tom Hark'

Have you ever seen a Scouser in the Kop? (x2)
Have you ever seen a Scouser
Ever seen a Scouser
Ever seen a Scouser in the Kop?
No chance!

Everton question the demographic make-up of local rivals.

♪: *'She'll Be Coming Round The Mountain'*

Shell suit for Christmas!
You got a shell suit for Christmas

Sung by opposition fans (also to Liverpool).

♪: *'Guantanamera'*

You're the Spurs (x2)
You're the Spurs of Merseyside

Sung by Arsenal fans.

Who can rob your houses? (x2)

Violate your gran? (x2)

Sell cocaine from an ice-cream van?

A Scouser can!

Sung by opposition fans (also to Liverpool).

🎼: *'The Candyman Can'*

Exeter

Can your chairman? (x2)

Can your chairman bend a spoon?

When magician Uri Geller was on the club board.

🎼: *'Bread Of Heaven'*

Falkirk

I bet your dad looks good on the dance floor!

To on-loan keeper Kasper Schmeichel about his dad, Peter, who was on *Strictly Come Dancing* at the time.

♪: *Arctic Monkeys' 'I Bet You Look Good On The Dance Floor'*

Fulham

We're forever reaching finals, reaching finals in Hamburg
We'll be on the beer, while they'll be stuck here
Watching *EastEnders* with their old dear
We'll be on the Reeperbahn, they'll still be in Dagenham
We're forever reaching finals, reaching finals in Hamburg!

Fulham fans respond to West Ham's 'We're Forever Blowing Bubbles' chant.

Oh Big Brede, Hangeland! Whoah Big Brede, Hangeland!

He jumps so high, Hangeland! You know that's no lie, Hangeland!

He's rock steady, Hangeland! When you see him on telly, Hangeland!

Oh Big Brede, Hangeland! Whoah Big Brede, Hangelaaaaaand

Tribute to giant Norwegian defender.

🎼: *Ram Jam's 'Black Betty'*

If you're sat in row Z
And the ball hits your head
That's Zamooooora

Sung before the striker hit form in 2009/10.

🎼: *'That's Amore'*

Frank, Frank, wherever you may be
Better change your locks cos we got your key
And soon we'll be back for your colour TV
Cos the writing on your wall says FFC

A few days after Frank Lampard's house was robbed.
♪: 'Lord Of The Dance'

Live round the corner
You only live round the corner

Chanted at Man United fans at Craven Cottage.
♪: 'Guantanamera'

From Stamford Bridge to Wem-ber-lee
You can stick the blue flag up your arse
Up your arse, up your arse
You can stick the blue flag up your arse

To their neighbours up the road at Chelsea, mocking the 'Blue Flag Flying High'
anthem.

Al Fayed, wo-ah-oh
Al Fayed, wo-ah-oh
He wants to be a Brit
And QPR are shit!

: *'Volare'*

If your chairman's got a passport, clap your hands (x2)
If your chairman's got a passport
Chairman's got a passport
Chairman's got a passport, clap your hands!

A reference to Al Fayed's unsuccessful application for a British passport.

: *'She'll Be Coming Round The Mountain'*

Where's your passport (x2)
Where's your passport, Al Fayed?
Hasn't got one
Never had one
You're a foreigner, Al Fayed

: *'Oh My Darling Clementine'*

Gateshead

Poor man's Evian

You're just a poor man's Evian

To Buxton supporters.

🎼: *'Guantanamera'*

Gillingham

E-I-E-I-E-I-O

Up the football league we go

We are the mighty Gillingham

We are the pride of Kent

And if you are a Millwall fan

You must be f***ing bent!

Most anti-Gillingham songs appear to be variations on a single theme:

All bling and Burberry
High teenage pregnancy
No father on the scene
All robbing cash machines!

 'La Donna E Mobile'

You can't read
You can't write
You wear gold and Nikes
You all come from Gillingham
And you are f***ing pikies

How much does your sister charge?

 'Go West'

Sing when you're palm-reading
You only sing when you're palm-reading

 'Guantanamera'

You can shove your lucky heather up your arse (x2)
You can shove your lucky heather
Shove your lucky heather
You can shove your lucky heather up your arse

🎼: *'She'll Be Coming Round the Mountain'*

Where's your caravan? (x2)

🎼: *'Where's Your Mama Gone?'*

Grimsby Town

We piss on your fish and chips

Grimsby town respond to weekly taunts about being a town full of chip shops, fish-shaggers, etc.

🎼: *'Go West'*

And for their friends in Yorkshire …

There's only one Peter Sutcliffe
One Peter Sutcliffe!

Yorkshire Ripper is our friend
Is our friend, is our friend
Yorkshire Ripper is our friend
He kills Yorkies!

♪: *'London Bridge Is Falling Down'*

With Grimsby now a non-league side, grounds have been a poorer place without the following:

You're shit and you smell of fish (x10)

And

You're fish and you smell of shit (x10)

♪: *'Go West'*

Sing when you're fishing
You only sing when you're fishing

♪: *'Guantanamera'*

Fish! Fish! Fish f***ers!

Hartlepool United

Nice ground, no fans

Taunt to Darlington about empty seats in their flash new 'Arena'.

🎼: *'Big Ben Chimes'*

Hearts

We're from the capital
You're from a shitehole

Welcoming visitors to Edinburgh.

🎼: *'La Donna E Mobile'*

Glasgow Rangers (x2)
You're not fit to wear the sash!

🎼: *'Bread Of Heaven'*

Tis the season to be jolly
Tra la la la la la la la la
Romanov's a f***ing wally
Tra la la la la la la la la ...

Hearts toast their controversial owner.

I was born under a Union Jack (x2)
Do you know where hell is?
Hell is Easter Road
Heaven is Tynecastle
Where the Hibees shite their load

♪: *'I Was Born Under A Wandering Star'*

We're going up, you're going down
We're going to wreck your f***ing town
We're going to rape, we're going to pillage
We're going to wreck your f***ing village

♪: *'Knick Knack Paddy Whack'*

Supercalifragilistic Devidas Cesnauskis

Supercalifragilistic Devidas Cesnauskis

Even though he's not our player, he's just on loan from Kaunas

Supercalifragilistic Devidas Cesnauskis

Hailing the Lithuanian.

🎼: *Mary Poppins' song*

Ten f***ing Hibees sitting on the wall (x2)

And if one f***ing Hibee should accidentally fall

There'll be nine f***ing Hibees sitting on the wall etc

Etc...

🎼: *'Ten Green Bottles'*

Jingle bells, jingle bells

Jingle all the way

Oh what fun it is to f**k

The Hibs on New Year's Day, eh!

Hibernian

Are you Woolworths? (x2)

Are you Woolworths in disguise?

Taunting Hearts over their financial plight.

𝄞: *'Bread Of Heaven'*

Sing at your weddings!

You only sing at your weddings!

To Gretna, now sadly demised.

𝄞: *'Guantanamera'*

Come on over to our place

Hey you, we'll give you the virus

We've got AIDS and hepatitis

So come on over tonight

Sung in response to opposition chants about Edinburgh being the drugs and HIV capital of Scotland.

𝄞: *The Drifters' 'Come On Over To My Place'*

You rake through your buckets for something to eat
You find a dead rat and you call it fresh meat
In your Gorgie slums!

Gorgie being an Edinburgh district and home to Hearts' Tynecastle ground.

Huddersfield Town

Crying on the telly

We saw you crying on the telly

To Leeds United fans after watching their tear-soaked players getting relegated.

♭: 'Guantanamera'

Those were the days, my friend
We thought they'd never end
We won the League three times in a row
We won the FA Cup
And then we f***ed it up
We are the Town, oh yes, we are the Town

Hull City

Have you ever seen a Tiger f**k a fish (x2)
Have you ever seen a Tiger
Ever seen a Tiger
Have you ever seen a Tiger f**k a fish

Tigers fans greeting their friends from Grimsby.

♭: *'She'll Be Coming Round The Mountain'*

You're not English (x2)
You're not English any more

To Arsenal's team of eleven foreigners.

♭: *'Bread Of Heaven'*

Silverware
We don't care
We follow City everywhere

♭: *'Tom Hark'*

He came from Bolton with a lack of knowledge

He studied management at Allardyce College

That's where I ... caught his eye

He told me that he was a manager

I said: 'In that case you'd better come and manage us'

He said: 'Fine'

And then, in three seasons' time

He said: 'I want to take you to the Vauxhall Conference

I want to do whatever Grimsby do

I want to sign lots of shitty players

I want to watch this club slide out of view

And hoof and hoof and hoof

Because ...

There's nothing left to do ...'

A witty rendition of Pulp's 'Common People' for former manager Phil Brown.

One bridge

You've only got one bridge ...

Sung by opposition fans.

𝄞: 'Blue Moon'

You can shove your f***ing ferries up your arse (x2)

You can shove your f***ing ferries

Shove your f***ing ferries

You can shove your f***ing ferries up your arse!

Sung by opposition fans

&: *'She'll Be Coming Round The Mountain'*

Inverness Caledonian Thistle

Are you on? (x2)

Are you on your holidays?

Highland team's surprise at seeing some visiting fans at their remote northern outpost

&: *'Bread Of Heaven'*

Ipswich Town

You mean f**k all to us (over and over)

Ipswich put Essex neighbours Colchester United in their place.

♪: *'La Donna E Mobile'*

Oh I'd rather be a farmer than a thief (x2)
Oh I'd rather be a farmer
Rather be a farmer
Oh I'd rather be a farmer than a thief!
F**k off!

To Liverpool and Everton fans. Also sung by Norwich.

♪: *'She'll Be Coming Round The Mountain'*

Did the ripper? (x2)
Did the ripper get your mum?

Opposition fans after deaths of five prostitutes in the town (also to Leeds).

♪: *'Bread Of Heaven'*

Where's your cattle gone?

Opposition fans at the height of the foot-and-mouth crisis (also to Norwich, Carlisle, etc.)

♪: *'Where's Your Mama Gone?'*

You're shit and you can't cook eggs (*ad infinitum*)

To Delia Smith for being a Norwich City director as well as Britain's most famous cook.

♪: *'Go West'*

Oi can't read and Oi can't write
But that don't really ma-er
Cos Oi come from Ipswich Town
Oi can drive a tractor
Oi can plough and milk a cow
And drive a great big mower
But the thing that Oi like best
Is being a potato grower
Oo-ar, oo-ar to be a Suffolk boy

To which the opposition reply with a cheery ...

Sing when you're farming

You only sing when you're farming

𝄞: *'Guantanamera'*

Kilmarnock

Oh I'd rather be a brush than be a Combe (x2)

Oh I'd rather be a brush

Rather be a brush

Rather be a brush than be a Combe!

Aberdeen fans to Kilmarnock keeper Alan Combe.

Leeds United

You don't know what you're doing! (over and over)

Leeds fans at Derby to a supporter who proposed to his girlfriend on the pitch.

We love sex, drugs and sausage rolls
But nothing compares to Beckford's goals

Before the striker moved to Everton.

We're not famous (x2)
We're not famous any more

Elland Road get mournful.

𝄞: *'Bread Of Heaven'*

Twelve more points to go
Twelve more points to zero

Sung after first win saw Leeds begin to wipe out their fifteen points deduction penalty.

𝄞: *'One Man Went To Mow'*

We filled your ground for you
(repeat till bored)

To smaller clubs with a low turn-out.

𝄞: *'La Donna E Mobile'*

A hundred years
You've won f**k all

To most of their opponents in League One.

🎼: *'Tom Hark'*

What the f**k? (x2)
What the f**k is going on?

Fans querying the goings-on in the boardroom as Leeds slid down the league and went bust.

🎼: *'Bread of Heaven'*

You've got more toes than us

To Burnley fans. When bored of toes, replace with eyes/thumbs, etc.

🎼: *'La Donna E Mobile'*

Your army's shit
And so are you

To Partizan Belgrade fans in UEFA Cup during Balkan crisis.

🎼: *'Tom Hark'*

Leeds, Leeds, wherever you may be
You are stuck in Division Three
You won't win a cup, you won't win a shield
Your biggest game is Huddersfield

Opposition fans bask in Leeds' plummeting fortunes.

♪: 'Lord Of The Dance'

Leicester City

He's big
He's round
He's six feet underground
Brian Clough, Brian Clough

Leicester taunt local rivals Derby and Forest about the glory days under the great man.

You're dead, and you know you are

And

Elvis, give us a song

Elvis, Elvis give us a song

To Leicester's Elvis Hammond.

Always shit on the red side of the Trent

Da da da, da da da, da da da

Forest are total shit

When you think of it

So always shit on

The red side of the Trent

𝄞: *'Always Look On The Bright Side of Life'*

Leyton Orient

You all shop at (x2)

You all shop at JJB

To Millwall.

𝄞: *'Bread Of Heaven'*

We can see you (x2)

We can see you washing up!

Swindon fans to the occupants of the flats overlooking Leyton Orient's Brisbane Road ground.

𝄞: *'Bread Of Heaven'*

Lincoln City

Mary had a little lamb
Who played in goal a lot
It let the ball go through its legs
So now it's in the pot

Liverpool

He's red
He's sound
He's banned from every ground
Carra's dad! Carra's dad!

Liverpool fans salute Jamie Carragher's father.

Cilla wants her teeth back (x2)
La-la-la, la-la-la

Liverpool fans to big-toothed Brazilian Ronaldinho.

Fat Robbie Savage
You're just a fat Robbie Savage!

And

Fat Paris Hilton
You're just a fat Paris Hilton!

Arsenal fans to Liverpool's blond-haired Ukrainian, Andriy Voronin.

🎼: 'Guantanamera'

He's big
He's red
His feet stick out the bed
Peter Crouch! Peter Crouch!

Liverpool fans remind their gangly six-foot-seven striker of his problems in the bedroom.

Pongolle, Pongolle
Sinama-Pongolle
He's got no song
Cos his name's too long
Sinama-Pongolle

Liverpool fans sing a farewell song to the Spain-bound French striker.

𝄞 *'Hooray! Hooray! It's A Holi-holiday'*

He's Scouse
He's sound
He'll hit you with a pound
Carragher! Carragher!

After the Reds defender threw a coin back in to the crowd at Arsenal.

Dirk Kuyt, as good as he may be
Hit every branch on the ugly tree
Like Fowler, Crouch and Craig Bellamy
Dirk Kuyt's boss but he's f***ing ugly

𝄞: *'Lord Of The Dance'*

Please don't look too surprised
When you're scythed from behind
By Traoré

If you get round the back
And you're suddenly hacked
That's Traoré

Yes his footwork is nice
Just like Bambi on ice
That's Traoré

Tribute to accident-prone French defender Djimi Traoré.

𝄞: *'That's Amore'*

He's quick, he's red
He talks like Father Ted
Robbie Keane! Robbie Keane!

Liverpool to the Irish striker.

Have you ever? (x2)
Have you ever seen your cock?

Man United fans point Liverpool manager Rafa Benitez to the salad bar.

𝄞: *'Bread Of Heaven'*

It's neat, it's weird
It's Rafa's goatee beard

Home fans salute Benitez's facial hair.

Fat Spanish waiter!
You're just a fat Spanish waiter!

Sung by opposition fans to Rafa Benitez.

𝄞: *'Guantanamera'*

Thursday nights, Channel 5!

Man United fans remind Liverpool about playing in the Europa League.

𝄞: *'Tom Hark'*

Feed the Scousers – let them know it's Christmas time

The opposition remind home fans (also to Everton) of the grinding poverty in which they live.

𝄞: *'Do They Know It's Christmas?'*

Macclesfield Town

You can shove your Yorkshire puddings up your arse
(x2)
You can shove your Yorkshire puddings
Shove your Yorkshire puddings
You can shove your Yorkshire puddings up your arse!

𝄞: *'She'll Be Coming Round The Mountain'*

Manchester City

U-N-I-

T-E-D

That spells f***ing debt to me

With a knick knack paddy whack

Give a dog a bone

Ocean Finance on the phone

Man City laugh at their poor neighbours.

We all live in a Robbie Fowler house

Robbie Fowler house, a Robbie Fowler house

Hailing the property tycoon.

𝄞: *'Yellow Submarine'*

Who's that crying at Old Trafford?

Who's that begging at the bank?

It's the Glazers and their clan, tearing up their master plan

Thank f**k we got the Sheikh and not the Yank

Debt-free City question Man United's liquidity.

𝄞: *'We All Follow'*

Sven, Sven, wherever you may be
You are the boss of Man City
You can shag my wife, on our settee
If we win the cup at Wem-ber-lee

To manager Sven-Göran Eriksson.
♪: *'Lord Of The Dance'*

You're supposed (x2)
You're supposed to have a neck

Sung by visitors to City's Craig Bellamy.
♪: *'Bread Of Heaven'*

We're the pride of (x2)
We're the pride of Manchester
You're the pride of Singapore

A dig at United's commercial enterprises in the Far East.
♪: *'Bread Of Heaven'*

Would you like another Stella, Georgie Best? (x2)
Would you like another Stella
Cos your face is turning yella
Would you like another Stella, Georgie Best?

Would you like another Bud Ice, Georgie Best? (x2)
Would you like another Bud Ice
Cos your face is turning jaundice
Would you like another Bud Ice, Georgie Best?

Would you like another whisky, Georgie Best? (x2)
Would you like another whisky
And fall like Emile Heskey
Would you like another whisky, Georgie Best?

Would you like another Becks, Georgie Best? (x2)
Would you like another Becks
You'll be pissing in your keks
Would you like another Becks, Georgie Best?

Would you like a Newcy Brown, Georgie Best? (x2)

Would you like a Newcy Brown

You'll soon be six foot down

Would you like a Newcy Brown, Georgie Best?

City fans showing their sympathy for the chronic alcohol problems of United legend George Best.

♪: *'She'll Be Coming Round The Mountain'*

Manchester United

Park, Park

Wherever you may be

You eat dogs in your home country

It could be worse, you could be Scouse

Eating rats in your council house!

To South Korean international Ji-Sung Park.

♪: *'Lord Of The Dance'*

And just in case he didn't get the joke first time round ...

He'll shoot, he'll score
He'll eat your Labrador

And just in case he forgets ...

Ten Alsatians walking down the street
Ten Alsatians walking down the street
And if Ji-Sung Park should want something to eat
There'll be nine Alsatians walking down the street etc

♪: *'Ten Green Bottles'*

This is what it's like to be City
This is what it's like to be small
This is what it's like to be a team that wins f**k all

To losing opposition teams.

♪: *Inspiral Carpets' 'This Is How It Feels'*

Kaka, wherever you may be
Have you heard of Man City?
Don't go there, it'll end in tears
They've not won a trophy in thirty years

Man United fans persuade Kaka to go for Real Madrid instead.
𝄞: *'Lord Of The Dance'*

City, wherever you may be
Wanted Kaka but got Bellamy
Owned by t**ts who haven't got a clue
You'll win f**k all like you always do.

𝄞: *'Lord Of The Dance'*

Nemanja, wo-ah-oh
He comes from Serbia
He'll f***ing murder ya

Tribute to centre-back Nemanja Vidic.
𝄞: *'Volare'*

United fans have produced dozens of verses to the song 'Oh, City Is A Massive Club' over the years to taunt their neighbours. To the tune of 'He's Got The Whole World In His Hands':

They've got Curly Watts as a celebrity fan (x3)
…

They had Ryan Giggs on schoolboy forms (x3)
…

They tried to sign Geoff Thomas and he turned 'em down (x3)
…

They won the Shamrock Trophy in '92 (x3)
…

They've got Bernard Manning as their fattest fan (x3)
…

They've got exec boxes with a balcony (x3)
…

They had a chairman and a manager that wore a wig (x3)
…

They've got the Gallagher brothers in the stands (x3)
…

They invade their pitch when they win three points (x3)

...

They do a lap of honour when they win the toss (x3)

...

They sing racist chants cos they've got no class (x3)

...

They've got fifty-four players but they're no f***ing good (x3)

...

They've got a gypsy curse on their massive pitch (x3)

...

They have a derby match with Macclesfield (x3)

...

They go to Wrexham and Cardiff on Euro-aways (x3)

...

They empty Stockport when they play at home (x3)

...

They've had seventeen managers in twenty years (x3)

...

They're the only team to come from Manchester (x3)

Since City beat United my true love sent to me:

European Champions

Eleven years of glory

Ten years in Europe

Nine goals past Ipswich

Eight–one at Forest

Seven past the Cockneys

Six title trophies

Five–nil wins!

Four FA Cups

Treble Ninety-Nine

Two Doubles

And an Eric Cantona

🎼: *'Twelve Days Of Christmas'*

Do you need? (x2)

Do you need a lift home?

Arsenal fans at Old Trafford.

In the town where I was born
There's a team we all adore
But there's a team that's f***ing shite
And they play in blue and white
Singing ...
City's going down like a Russian submarine
A Russian submarine, a Russian submarine

: 'Yellow Submarine'

He's fat
He's Scouse
He's probably robbed your house
Rooney! Rooney!

On your Yorkshire farms
You bother the lambs in the long grass
You'd rather shag sheep than a fit normal lass
On your Yorkshire farms!

From the old days when Leeds were regular visitors.

: 'In Your Northern Slums'

Viva Da Silva! Viva Da Silva!

When they're on the pitch

We don't know which is which

Viva Da Silva!

Admitting confusion over the Brazilian identical twins Fabio and Rafael da Silva.

🎼: *'Viva Las Vegas'*

Who's that slave they call Ronaldo

Who's that slave we once adored

With shackles round his feet

On a hundred grand a week

Dozy c**t, you should think before you speak

In the wake of Ronaldo agreeing with comments from FIFA President Sepp Blatter that he was a slave at United, blocking his move to Real Madrid.

Mansfield Town

We're shit and we know we are (x4)

: *'Go West'*

Marine FC

There's only one Michael Jackson, one Michael Jackson
There used to be two
But now there's just you
Walking in a Jackson Neverland

In honour of the Marine FC midfielder following the death of the US pop star.

Middlesbrough

Shearer, wherever you may be
We all laughed when you f***ed your knee
Bellamy was right, you're f***ing shite
You won f**k all in black and white

Boro taunt the great Geordie.

♪: 'Lord Of The Dance'

They're here, they're there
They're every f***ing where
Wisey's eyes!

Querying Dennis Wise's eyeball arrangement.

A wonderful way to spend Valentine's Day
Watching Joe Kinnear pass away

Middlesborough respond to news that Newcastle manager has had a heart attack.

We drink X
We drink Brown
We're going to wreck your f***ing town
With pissed up Boro fans running all around
We'll kill you all outside your ground

♪ 'Knick Knack Paddy Whack'

Millwall

Who's the pervert? (x2)

Who's the pervert on the wall?

To policeman filming them.

𝄞: *'Bread Of Heaven'*

Your mum is an Essex slag (x4)

To Southend.

𝄞: *'Go West'*

If we lose, if we fail

We take it out on British Rail

Wreck the train! (x2)

We're the best-behaved supporters in the league (x2)

We're the best-behaved supporters

Best-behaved supporters

Best-behaved supporters in the league

We're a right bunch of bastards when we lose (x2)
We're a right bunch of bastards
Right bunch of bastards
We're a right bunch of bastards when we lose

'She'll Be Coming Round The Mountain'

You'll never make the station! (over and over)
And ...
Let's go smash the town up! (x2)
La la la, la la la

We've got central heating! (x2)
La la la, la la la
To teams from poor areas.

We hate Tuesday
And we hate Tuesday
We are the Tuesday-haters!
In response to Sheffield United fans singing 'We hate Wednesday', etc.

You're not scary any more!

Yeovil fans to Millwall.

MK Dons

Who did you? (x2)
Who did you support before?

🎼: *'Bread Of Heaven'*

And ...

What's it like? (x2)
What's it like to steal a team?

Opposition fans question the football fidelity of the MK Dons' (formerly Wimbledon) support.

To which the Dons' fans reply ...

Sit down or we'll steal your club

🎼: *'Go West'*

Or ...

Beaten by a franchise!
You're getting beaten by a franchise!

𝄞: *'Guantanamera'*

Staines, Staines, wherever you may be
We've got the proper Ali G
And he'll score more goals than all of AFC
So stick them up your Punani

MK Dons toast Canadian striker Ali Gerba.

𝄞: *'Lord Of The Dance'*

Easter's better than Christmas!

MK Dons fans after Jermaine Easter scored on Boxing Day.

We got a big black Willy in our goal (x3)
And the Dons go marching on, on, on!

To Willy Gueret.

𝄞: *'He's Got The Whole World In His Hands'*

Look like a Wotsit
You look like a Wotsit!

Southampton fans to MK Dons' flame-haired captain Dean Lewington.

 *'Guantanamera'*

Motherwell

Well I've been a muff-diver for many a year
I spent all my money on muff-diving gear
From goggles to flippers and an oxygen tank
If I cant have a muff-dive I'll just have a wank
And it's Moth-er-well
Moth-er-well FC!
They're by far the greatest team the world has ever
seen

'No Nay Never'/'The Wild Rover'

We are the Well – can't you hear us? (x2)

Walking along, singing a song

Shitting on the Hibees all the way

Newcastle United

We are the Geordies

Obese of the North

We all hate salads and healthfoods of course

We all eat pasties and Mars bars and chops

And we all wear extra-large tops

The Geordies confirm suspicions about their diet.

𝄞: *'Cock Of The North'*

He's fat! He's round!

He swears like Chubby Brown

Joe Kinnear! Joe Kinnear!

In praise of the portly, foul-mouthed gaffer.

Ashley, wherever you may be

Selling shit in JJB

You're big and you're fat

You cockney t**t

Now f**k off home to your council flat

Newcastle to unpopular owner Mike Ashley.

𝄞: *'Lord Of The Dance'*

Also ...

Taxi for Ashley!

You're not yodelling (x2)

You're not yodelling any more

Newcastle fans after scoring at FC Zurich.

𝄞: *'Bread Of Heaven'*

When Toon go up, to lift the FA cup – we'll be dead

Newcastle fans laugh at their team's lack of success.

Newcastle fans have many verses with which to taunt their Sunderland neighbours. To the tune of 'He's Got The Whole World In His Hands':

You get a free season ticket in a happy meal (x3)

...

Adults for a fiver, kids go free (x3)

...

You get cheesy chips for just a quid (x3)

...

They've got 27,000 empty seats (x3)

...

They've got Steve Cram, celebrity fan (x3)

...

It took twenty-eight years to beat us at home (x3)

...

Oh Sunderland's a massive club... are they f**k? (x3)

Fifty years! We've won f**k all!

We're shite and we're sick of it (x3)

Newcastle do self-deprecation.

♪: *'Go West'*

He's slow
He's old
He's ninety-six years old
Nicky Butt! Nicky Butt!

He's loyal
He's class
He'll put you on your arse
Nicky Butt! Nicky Butt!

Pick your Joey Barton favourite, sung by opposition fans, following the midfielder's jail sentence for assault and affray:

Shagged in the showers
He's getting shagged in the showers

𝄞: *'Guantanamera'*

Shit in a bucket
He has to shit in a bucket

𝄞: *'Guantanamera'*

Oh Joey's arse (x2)
Is always full (x2)
Oh Joey's arse is always full
Full of B, C and D wing
Oh Joey's arse is always full

 'When The Saints Go Marching In'

Glory, glory, hallelujah
Joey's gonna take it up his brown star
Keegan isn't very happy
Cos Joey's gonna need a nappy
And he ain't gonna play no more! More! More!

Stayed on the telly
You should've stayed on the telly

Liverpool fans to BBC pundit Shearer during his brief reign as manager of Newcastle.

 'Guantanamera'

Shit f***ing barcode
You're just a shit f***ing barcode

Visitors take a swipe at the famous black and white stripes.

𝄞: *'Guantanamera'*

Banked with the Woolwich
You should have banked with the Woolwich

Sung by opposition fans after sponsors Northern Rock went bust.

𝄞: *'Guantanamera'*

Have you ever seen the Geordies win the league? (x2)
Have you ever seen the Geordies
Ever seen the Geordies
Have you ever seen the Geordies win the league?

Sung by opposition fans.

𝄞: *'She'll Be Coming Round The Mountain'*

Northampton Town

Singing aye aye yippy yippy aye

F**k the Posh!

Singing aye aye yippy yippy aye

F**k the Posh!

Singing aye aye yippy

Aye aye yippy

Aye aye yippy yippy aye

F**k the Posh!

One for Peterborough – perhaps more amusing to sing than to listen to.

Norwich City

One Gordon Ramsay

There's only one Gordon Ramsay

Opposition fans to Norwich fans.

𝄞: 'Guantanamera'

You can shove your f***ing saucepans up your arse! (x2)

You can shove your f***ing saucepans

Shove your f***ing saucepans

Shove your f***ing saucepans up your arse

Opposition fans offer some practical kitchen advice to the club's joint majority shareholder/cook Delia Smith.

♪: 'She'll Be Coming Round the Mountain'

Norwich fans: You've got a Russian crook, we've got a super cook

Chelsea fans: We've got Abramovich, you've got a crazy b***h

Shall we burn you? (x2)

Shall we burn you just in case?

Opposition fans during foot-and-mouth crisis.

♪: 'Bread Of Heaven'

Nottingham Forest

Guy, Guy, Guy Moussi

You eat frogs in your home country

But it could be worse

You could be a Ram

An ugly inbred shagging your mam!

Reminding French midfielder of his luck in not being a Derby fan.

🎼: *'Lord Of The Dance'*

In the town where I was born

There's a team we all adore

But there's a team that's f***ing shite

And they play in black and white

Singing ...

County's going down like a Russian submarine

A Russian submarine, a Russian submarine

🎼: *'Yellow Submarine'*

Raddy, Raddy Majewski
He fixed burst pipes in his own country
Now he's over here, nicking English jobs
Scoring goals with his shots and lobs!

Saluting the arrival of the Polish midfielder.

♪: *'Lord Of The Dance'*

You're not famous (x2)
You're not famous any more

Sung by visitors (also to Leeds).

♪: *'Bread Of Heaven'*

Robin Hood, Robin Hood, riding through the glen
Robin Hood, Robin Hood, and his merry men
Steals from the rich, gives to the poor

Pause

Silly c**t, silly c**t, silly c**t

Sung by visiting fans to the city of Nottingham.

♪: *'Robin Hood, Riding Through The Glen'*

We'd rather bomb Derby than Iraq (x2)

We'd rather bomb Derby

Rather bomb Derby

We'd rather bomb Derby than Iraq

♪: *'She'll Be Coming Round The Mountain'*

Notts County

You'll never bash the Bishop

Tribute to midfielder Neal Bishop.

Juve, Juve
It's just like watching Juve (x3)

The two teams have a black-and-white striped shirt in common.

♪: *'Blue Moon'*

Oldham Athletic

Give us a T!
Give us an I!
Give us a T!
Give us an S!
What do you do with 'em?
'Old 'em! 'Old 'em!

Breeze Hill
It's just like watching
Breeze Hill (x3)

Funny take on 'It's Just Like Watching Brazil' – Breeze Hill is a school near Oldham's Boundary Park ground.

🎼: *'Blue Moon'*

Oxford United

Blue moon

You got promoted too soon

Now you're going back down

Conference is coming to town

Sung to teams recently promoted from the Conference (now that Oxford are out of it again, that is).

When the red, red robin comes bob-bob-bobbing along

Shoot the bastard, shoot the bastard

One for Oxford's friends down the road at Swindon, aka the Robins.

The following are sung by opposition fans:

You can shove your f***ing uni up your arse (x2)

You can shove your f***ing uni

Shove your f***ing uni

You can shove your f***ing uni up your arse

And ...

You can shove your f***ing boat race up your arse (x2)
You can shove your f***ing boat race
Shove your f***ing boat race
You can shove your f***ing boat race up your arse

&: 'She'll Be Coming Round The Mountain'

Sing when you're rowing
You only sing when you're rowing

&: 'Guantanamera'

You'll never win the boat race (x10)

Partick Thistle

All I want is a twelve-inch dick

A season ticket for Partick

A Killie fan

To punch and kick

Oh, wouldn't it be lovely

♪: 'Wouldn't It Be Loverly'

I know a lassie

A bonnie, bonnie lassie

She's as tight as the paper on the wall

She's got legs like a spider

I'd love to f***ing ride her

Mary from Maryhill

I was just about to hump her

When her tits fell out her jumper

And her knees were banging off the wall
She's got a big fat belly
She is awfully scaly
Mary from Maryhill

If you want to go to heaven when you die
You must wear a Thistle scarf and tie
You must wear a Thistle bonnet
With 'F**k the Old Firm' on it
If you want to go to heaven when you die
Singing I'm no a Killie I'm a Jag
Singing I'm no a Killie I'm a Jag
Singing I'm no a Killie
Don't be so f***ing silly
Singing I'm no a Killie, I'm a Jag
Thank f**k!

For uninitiated English football followers, the Jags is Partick's nickname, while Killie refers to rivals Kilmarnock.

♪: *'She'll Be Coming Round The Mountain'*

Peterborough United

Darren, call your dad
Darren, Darren, call your dad!

Visiting fans suggest Peterborough boss Darren Ferguson gives Sir Alex a bell for some tactical advice (now sung at Preston).

We've got MacAnthony
You live in poverty

Posh fans celebrate being bought by Marbella-based property entrepreneur Darragh MacAnthony.

𝄞: *'La Donna E Mobile'*

Plymouth Argyle

Get your growler out

To female steward.

𝄞: *'Where's Your Mama Gone?'*

Our dockyard shed (x2)

Is bigger than this (x2)

We've got a nuclear sub

Our dockyard shed is bigger than this

Sung at Arsenal's new Emirates Stadium.

♪: *'When The Saints Go Marching In'*

He's big

He's fat

He's had a heart attack

Joe Kinnear! Joe Kinnear!

Joe Kinnear's a wanker

He wears a wanker's hat

And when he watches football

He has a heart attack

Some Argyle fans never quite forgave the former Wimbledon and Luton manager for some disparaging comments he made about their team and were tickled pink when the man collapsed.

♪: *'My Old Man's A Dustman'*

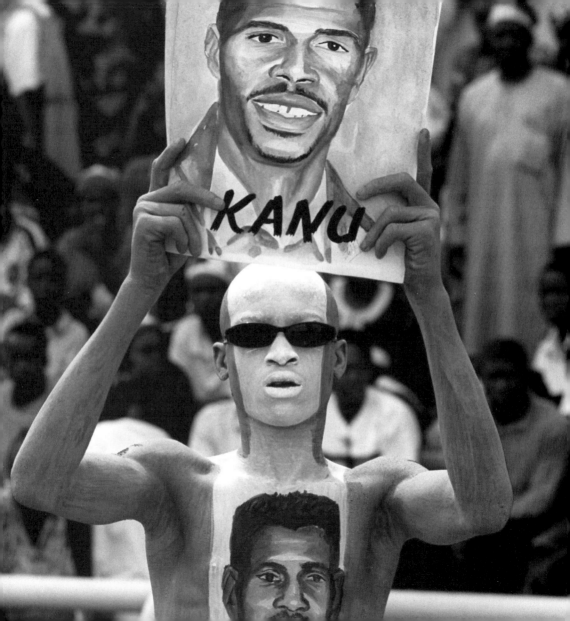

You can stick your Cornish pasties up your arse (x2)

You can stick your Cornish pasties

Stick your Cornish pasties

You can stick your Cornish pasties up your arse

A favourite for opposition fans.

𝄞: *'She'll Be Coming Round The Mountain'*

Portsmouth

He's big

He's black

He's had a heart attack

He's Kanu! He's Kanu!

Portsmouth fans remind their star Nigerian striker Nwankwo Kanu of his medical history.

We've got the whole world in our team

Hailing their overseas team.

𝄞: *'He's Got The Whole World In His Hands'*

Walk on, walk on

With a hedgehog up your arse

You'll never walk again

You'll never walk again

Portsmouth fans get surreal as they deride the Liverpool anthem.

King Kanu, Kanu

He's older than me and you

His real age is sixty-two

King Kanu, Kanu

𝄞: *'Que Sera'*

Sing when you're ringing

You only sing when you're ringing

And

You're not ringing any more!

Arsenal fans to the top-hatted, tattooed, crazy-guy Pompey fan with the bell.

𝄞: *'Guantanamera'*

Randy, buy 'em a roof
Randy, Randy, buy 'em a roof!

Villa fans in uncovered stand at Portsmouth turn to their rich US owner Randy Lerner when it starts to rain.

I'd rather have a dinghy than a Kanu

Arsenal fans to Portsmouth's Nigerian striker.

Port Vale

You're supposed to (x2)
You're supposed to be a gnome!

Port Vale fans to a small referee.

𝄞: *'Bread Of Heaven'*

Christmas time, valium and wine
Children indulging in serious crime
Mum on the heroin, and Dad snorting coke
Christmas is magic when you support Stoke

𝄞: *Cliff Richard's 'Mistletoe And Wine'*

In the town where I was born

There was a team

We go to see

And we had ten pints of ale

Before we went to see the Vale

We all piss in a red and white hat

A red and white hat

A red and white hat

The red and white hat being the property of neighbours Stoke City.

🎼: *'Yellow Submarine'*

Preston North End

Always look on the Turf Moor for shite

PNE fans greet their friends on arrival at Burnley.

🎼: *'Always Look On The Bright Side Of Life'*

Christmas time

Heroin and wine

Kids indulging in petty crime

Your mum is a Mack-head

Your dad is a tool

A typical family from Blackpool

Preston show some festive spirit to their friends on the coast.

♪: 'Mistletoe And Wine'

Who's that jumping off the pier?

Who's that drowning in the sea?

It's Ian and the boys, making such a f***ing noise

Cos they can't beat the famous PNE

Sea-sea-seaside shit! (x2)

Preston greet their chums from Blackpool.

♪: 'We All Follow'

Blackpool Tower is falling down
Falling down, falling down
Blackpool Tower is falling down
Poor old Blackpool
Build it up in blue and white
Blue and white, blue and white
Build it up in blue and white
Poor old Blackpool

🎼: *'London Bridge Is Falling Down'*

Queen's Park

One team in Glasgow
There's only one team in Glasgow

Queen's Park forget about Celtic and Rangers.

Queens Park Rangers

Strawberry blond, you're having a laugh! (*ad infinitum*)

QPR fans to ginger midfielder Ben Watson after he went to West Brom.

♪: *'Tom Hark'*

If you can't talk proper, shut your mouths (x2)
If you can't talk proper
Can't talk proper
If you can't talk proper, shut your mouths

Sung to northern clubs.

♪: *'She'll Be Coming Round The Mountain'*

One size, Fitz Hall!
One size, Fitz Hall!

♪: *'Big Ben Chimes'*

Sack in the morning
You'll get the sack in the morning

West Brom fans when QPR's fifth manager of the season, Neil Warnock, was introduced to the home crowd shortly before his first match.

: *'Guantanamera'*

We could buy your (x2)
We could buy your whole estate

Sung to clubs from supposedly deprived areas.

: *'Bread Of Heaven'*

Town full of bombers
You're just a town full of bombers

Hull fans to QPR shortly after the 7 July bombings in London.

: *'Guantanamera'*

We've got Matt Connolly
You shag your family

Previously sung to Connolly's namesake Karl.

: *'La Donna E Mobile'*

Rangers

Deep-fry your vodka
We're gonna deep-fry your vodka

Rangers to St Petersburg in the 2008 UEFA Cup final.
♪: 'Guantanamera'

All things bright and beautiful
All creatures great and small
All things wise and wonderful
John Hartson ate them all

Rangers to Celtic fans about their beefy Welsh striker.

Sing in the Chapel
You only sing in the Chapel

To their Presbyterian friends.
♪: 'Guantanamera'

You can stick your Tartan Army up your arse (x2)

You can stick your Tartan Army

Stick your Tartan Army

You can stick your Tartan Army up your arse

🎼: *'She'll Be Coming Round The Mountain'*

Tell all the Tims you know

That their giros and Euros don't go

Oh you'll no need your shades

Or your bucket and spades

Inverness is as far as you'll go

Joy that Celtic (Tims) are out of Europe.

🎼: *'Que Sera'*

Paul le Guen

Is getting the sack

He lost the league

Before the clocks went back

Sung by Celtic fans after the brief tenure of the French manager at Rangers.

🎼: *'Tom Hark'*

Reading

You're Posh, but you're not Royal (x10)

Royal's fans taunt Peterborough, aka The Posh, about their lack of class.

🎼: *'Go West'*

He's young, he's flash
He fills the air with ash
Sigurdsson! Sigurdsson!

For their volcanic Icelandic midfielder.

Bill Oddie (x2)
Rub your beard all over my body

Reading welcome their celebrity fan and naturalist.

🎼: *Madonna's 'Erotica'*

You're so quiet (x2)
We think you're Aldershot

🎼: *'Bread Of Heaven'*

Rochdale

Does your wife? (x2)

Does your wife have woolly hair?

Sung to Welsh and Yorkshire teams, especially Halifax.

𝄞: *'Bread Of Heaven'*

On a similar theme to a similar audience ...

Always look in the fields for a wife

𝄞: *'Always Look On The Bright Side Of Life'*

Rotherham United

When I was young I had some sense

I bought a flute for twenty pence

The only tune that I could play was

'F**k The Blades And Sheffield Wednesday!'

Scunthorpe United

Who needs Mourinho
We've got our physio

Tribute to Nigel Adkins, the club physio who took over as manager after the departure of Brian Laws and led the club to promotion to the Championship.

♪: *'La Donna E Mobile'*

Sheffield United

He'll slash

He'll chop

He'll put you in his wok

Sun Jihai! Sun Jihai!

Fans greet China international following his transfer from Manchester City.

We're not singing (x2)

We're not singing any more

Sheffield United sample irony after going behind.

♭: *'Bread Of Heaven'*

You can shove your f***ing hotpot up your arse (x2)

You can shove your f***ing hotpot

Shove your f***ing hotpot

You can shove your f***ing hotpot up your arse

One for visitors from Lancashire.

♭: *'She'll Be Coming Round The Mountain'*

Shall we build a? (x2)

Shall we build a stand for you?

Sung to local rivals Rotherham, whose ground capacity is 11,500, and other smaller clubs.

🎼: *'Bread Of Heaven'*

Wednesday!

Whatever will you do?

You're going down to Division Two

And you won't win a cup

And you won't win a shield

And your next derby is Chest-er-field

Wednesday!

Whatever will you do?

You're going down to Division Two

And you can take your trumpet

And take your drum

And go and play with the Barnsley scum

A moving farewell for their city rivals with some tips for their musicians in the stands.

🎼: *'Lord Of The Dance'*

You fill up my senses

Like a gallon of Magnet

Like a packet of Woodbines

Like a good pinch of snuff

Like a night out in Sheffield

Like a greasy chip buttie

Like Sheffield United

Come fill me again!

𝄞: *'Annie's Song'*

Sheffield Wednesday

We got one stand bigger than your ground (x2)

We got one stand bigger

One stand bigger

We got one stand bigger than your ground!

Sung to virtually everyone in League One.

𝄞: *'She'll Be Coming Round The Mountain'*

You'll never lick the Beever

Sucking up to defender Mark Beevers.

Southampton

Hollow, Hollow, Hollow
Pompey's success is f***ing hollow
All that money they took
From that big Russian crook
And their stadium's still a shithole

Bale, Bale, wherever you may be
You shag sheep in your own country
It could be worse
Cos you could be a Skate
And take your own sister out on a date

Tribute to former full-back Gareth Bale from Wales (a Skate is a Pompey fan).

𝄞: 'Lord Of The Dance'

Swing Lowe

Swing Rupert Lowe

Swing him from Itchen Bridge

A gospel hymn to former chairman Rupert Lowe.

Southend United

Oh I do like to be beside the seaside

Oh I do like to be beside the sea

With a bucket and a spade and a f***ing hand grenade

Beside the seaside, beside the sea!

Oh Southend pier

Is longer than yours

Oh Southend pier is longer than yours

It's got some shops and a railway

Oh Southend pier is longer than yours

♪: 'When The Saints Go Marching In'

Oh, the grand old Duke of York
He had 10,000 men
None of them could kick a ball
So he sold them to Southend

Stockport County

Fake town, fake fans (over and over)

Sung to MK Dons.

𝄞: *'Big Ben Chimes'*

Stoke City

We support (x2)
We support our local team

Stoke to Man United and Chelsea.

𝄞: *'Bread Of Heaven'*

Who needs Robinho?
We've got Delap's throw

𝄞: 'La Donna E Mobile'

You are a rammer, a dirty rammer
You're only happy when making hay
Your mum's a nympho
Your dad's a scarecrow
Please don't take my tractor away

Sung to the Rams of Derby County.
𝄞: 'You Are My Sunshine'

Pulis is a tosser, he wears a baseball cap
He's only got one tactic, the f***ing t**t Delap
He throws from the left wing and he throws from the right
If he couldn't throw the ball
Stoke would be f***ing shite

Opposition fans wonder if Stoke have a plan B.
𝄞: 'My Old Man's A Dustman'

Sunderland

Niall Quinn's disco pants are the best
They go right from his arse to his chest
They are better than Adam and the Ants
Niall Quinn's disco pants

Surreal praise for the Irishman's clubbing gear.

Glory, glory, hallelujah!
Joey Barton, six months in the cooler
Joey thinks he's a big hitter
But now he takes it up the shitter
And he ain't gonna play no more,
more, more!

Sunderland fans react to the news that the
Newcastle midfielder has been jailed for assault.

He's big, he's thick
He's got a ginger dick
Paul McShane! Paul McShane!

Words of encouragement for the young Irish defender.

He's big, he's round
He weighs a million pound
Joe Kinnear! Joe Kinnear!

Swansea City

What's that coming over the hill
Is it the taxman? Is it the taxman?

To Cardiff after failure to pay their tax bill on time.

𝄞 *Automatic's 'Monster'*

Austin is our hero
He's solid as a rock
He plays in front of Willy
Who's got a massive cock

Swansea about centre-back Kevin Austin and keeper Willy Gueret.
𝄞: *'My Old Man's A Dustman'*

One–nil to the sheep shaggers (*ad infinitum*)

𝄞: *'Go West'*

We shag 'em
You eat 'em!

The Welsh side finally come clean.

I'm dreaming of a white Christmas
Just like the ones I used to know
When the Swans are flying
The Bluebirds are dying
And Davie Jones is wanking in the snow

Cheery festive greetings for their friends in Cardiff.

Swindon Town

What's it like? (x2)

What's it like to have no Cox?

Swindon fans to Northampton after the Robins beat them to the signing of Simon Cox. Sadly for the Swindon fans, he then moved on to West Brom.

♪: *'Bread Of Heaven'*

All things bright and beautiful

All creatures great and small

Swindon rule the West Country and Oxford rule f**k all

QPR fans to Swindon: Going down, going down, going down ...

Swindon fans: So are we, so are we, so are we ...

Swindon, Swindon, Ra! Ra! Ra!

Oxford, Oxford, Ha! Ha! Ha!

Bristol, Bristol, Ba! Ba! Ba!

Scousers, Scousers, where's my car?

Torquay United

You dirty northern bastards (*ad infinitum*)

Sung to all teams except Plymouth, even Exeter, to which they might hear the reply:

You can shove your Riviera up your arse (x2)

You can shove your Riviera

Shove your Riviera

You can shove your Riviera up your arse

𝄞: *'She'll Be Coming Round The Mountain'*

Have you ever? (x2)

Have you ever seen a beach?

To landlocked Midlands clubs.

𝄞: *'Bread Of Heaven'*

Tottenham Hotspur

Tributes to six-foot-seven Peter Crouch:

He's big! He's shit!
He can't fit in his kit
Peter Crouch! Peter Crouch!

He's tall! He's mad!
He dances like your dad
Peter Crouch! Peter Crouch!

Does the circus? (x2)
Does the circus know you're here?

𝄞: *'Bread Of Heaven'*

Peter Crouch is an oxymoron (repeat till bored)

𝄞: *'You're Going Home In A London Ambulance'*

Attack! Defend!
He'll eat man's best friend
Y. P. Lee! Y. P. Lee!

Reminding Korean left-back of the treats he's missing back home.

Fat Annie Lennox
You're just a fat Annie Lennox

Sung to West Ham's bleach-haired Dean Ashton.

♪: *'Guantanamera'*

One week in, three weeks out
Ledley is a tampon!

A reference to Ledley King's dodgy knees.

Shit Gary Neville
You're just a shit Gary Neville

To Gary's brother Phil Neville at Everton.

♪: *'Guantanamera'*

Shit Chas and Dave
You're just a shit Chas and Dave

Tottenham fans on spotting Man City fan Liam Gallagher in the ground.

🎼: *'Guantanamera'*

I'm only a poor little yiddo
I stand at the back of the Shelf
I go to the bar, to buy a lager
And only buy one for myself

Tottenham do irony.

He's only a poor little Gooner
He stands at the end of the Bank
He watches the Reds
The football he dreads
So he ends up having a wank

And the original version.

Tranmere Rovers

Don't be mistaken
Don't be misled
We are not Scousers
We're from Birkenhead
You can f**k your cathedral
And your pier head
Cos we are not Scousers
We're from Birkenhead

We hate Scousers
And we hate Scousers
We are the Scouser-haters!

Walsall

We are the pride of the Midlands
The Villa are scum
We hate the Wanderers
The Baggies and Brum
We are the Walsall
We are the best
We are the Saddlers
So f**k all the rest!

Small town in Poland
You're just a small town in Poland

Sung by opposition fans.

𝄞 'Guantanamera'

Watford

Sit down and read your books (over and over)

On a visit to the Arsenal 'library'.

𝄞: *'Go West'*

Aaa-gaa ... doo-doo-doo
We're the Watford wrecking crew
To the left, to the right
Luton Town are f***ing shite!

𝄞: *Black Lace's 'Agadoo'*

The Luton train came over the hill
The hill, the hill
The Luton train came over the hill
The hill, the hill
The Luton train came over the hill
The brakes failed and they all got killed
Singing, ha, ha, ha, ha, ha, ha

𝄞: *'The Runaway Train'*

West Bromwich Albion

Mulumbu – wo-ah-oh! (x2)

He was a refugee

But now he's quality

♪: *'Volare'*

Saw your mum (x2)

Saw your mum on Jeremy Kyle

West Brom fans to a fat, misbehaving Reading fan.

♪: *'Bread Of Heaven'*

You're shit and your tramp is dead

West Brom to Wolves in reference to the passing away of local character Fred the Ring Road Tramp.

♪: *'Go West'*

Lip up fatty-o, lip up fatty

Rooney, Rooney

A modern Midlands rendition of the Bad Manners classic.

Bernt Haas
Shouldn't light his farts
Bernt Haas
Shouldn't light his farts

West Brom fans to Swiss defender.

🎼: 'Go West'

Taylor is a turnip
He's got a turnip's head
He took the job at Villa
He must have been brain-dead

Do I not like this?
Do I not like that?
Everyone in England knows
He is a f***ing t**t

A touching welcome for the former Villa and Wolves boss.

🎼: 'My Old Man's A Dustman'

Shit f***ing deckchair
You're just a shit f***ing deckchair

Opposition fans have a go at the West Brom stripes.

𝄞: *'Guantanamera'*

West Ham United

Fat Maradona
You're just a fat Maradona

To former Hammer Carlos Tevez.

𝄞: *'Guantanamera'*

World Cup
We won the f***ing World Cup (x3)

A reference to the 1966 heroics of Moore, Peters and Hurst.

𝄞: *'Blue Moon'*

Vera's dead! (over and over)

At Man City after the death of *Coronation Street* character Vera Duckworth.

I remember Wembley
When West Ham beat West Germany
Martin one and Geoffrey three
And Bobby got the OBE!

You ate all your mates (x2)
You ate, you ate, you ate, you ate
You ate all your mates!

To an obese opposition fan surrounded by empty seats.

&: 'Knees Up Mother Brown'

You can shove your f***ing bubbles up
your arse (x2)
You can shove your f***ing bubbles
Shove your f***ing bubbles
You can shove your f***ing bubbles up
your arse!

Opposition fans when the Hammers roll out the
East End anthem 'I'm Forever Blowing Bubbles'.

&: 'She'll Be Coming Round The Mountain'

My one skin goes over my two skin

My two skin goes over my three

My three skin goes over my foreskin

Oh bring back my foreskin to me!

Bring back, bring back

Oh bring back my foreskin to me!

Generally reserved for the Hammers' London cousins up the road at Tottenham.

𝄞: *'My Bonnie Lies Over The Ocean'*

Wigan Athletic

Mum is a badger

Your mum is a badger

Tottenham fans to Wigan's two-tone Paul Scharner.

𝄞: *'Guantanamera'*

You can stick your f***ing rugby up your arse (x2)

𝄞: *'She'll Be Coming Round The Mountain'*

He's fast
He's slick
He's got a massive d**k
N'zogbia! N'zogbiaaaa!

A couple of ditties for their rugby league friends in this close-knit sporting community:

We come from Wigan
And we live in mudhuts
Ooh aah, ooh ooh aah
Ooh to be a Wiganer

Don't ask ...

They're stinky and they're smelly
They come from Scholes and Whelley
They haven't got a telly
The Wigan Warriors

𝄞: 'Addams Family'

Wimbledon

We are Wombles, we are Wombles
We are Wombles, from Plough Lane
We are Wombles, super Wombles
We are Wombles, we drink champagne

We drink champagne, we snort cocaine
We've got ladies over 'ere
You've got shit jobs, you shag your dogs
And your wife is on the game

We drink Campari, we drive Ferraris
We've got ladies over 'ere
You drink John Smiths, you're all blacksmiths
And your toilet's out the rear

We wear Gucci, we wear Armani
We've got cashmere over here

You've got shell suits, Wellington boots
And your fashion's soooooo last year

♪: *'Oh My Darling Clementine'*

Windsor & Eton

We've got Dave Tilbury
He'll paint your house for free
He quotes and estimates
He paints and decorates

Windsor & Eton for their tradesman defender Dave Tilbury.

♪: *'La Donna E Mobile'*

Wolverhampton Wanderers

Oh, the grand Old Duke of Brom
He had eleven men
He marched 'em up to the Premier League
And they came straight down again!
Cos when they were up, they were shit!
And now they are down, they are shit!
It doesn't matter if they're up or down
Cos they'll always be shit!

Tina, Tina, give us a wave!

To Portsmouth's David James, sporting a Tina Turner-style hair-do.

Bus stop in Aston
You're just a bus stop in Aston (*ad infinitum*)

To Birmingham fans.

♪: '*Guantanamera*'

Always shit on a Tesco carrier bag
La la la, la la la, la la la

An oblique reference to the strip of local rivals West Brom.

♪: *'Always Look On The Bright Side Of Life'*

Wrexham

We love Taboubi (x2)
We love Taboubi on a Saturday night

Welcoming French midfielder Hedi Taboubi.

♪: *T Rex's 'We Love To Boogie'*

I'm a bastard
I'm a bastard
I'm a bastard, yes I am
But I'd rather be a bastard
Than a f***ing Englishman

♪: *'Oh My Darling Clementine'*

We'll burn all your tables
We'll burn all your chairs
We'll burn all your children when sleeping upstairs
In your holiday homes

Wrexham boys give the English visitors a toasty warm welcome.

Oh fluffy sheep are wonderful
Oh fluffy sheep are wonderful
They are white, Welsh and fluffy
Oh fluffy sheep are wonderful

Responding to nasty English taunts about their relationship with Welshmen.
♪: *'When The Saints Go Marching In'*

Wycombe Wanderers

No Woodman – no cry

When Wycombe had Craig Woodman sent off.

Yeovil Town

Drink up your cider, drink up your cider

For tonight we'll be merry, merry be

We're on our way to Dover

To f**k in the clover

There's plenty more cider in the jar

We all came on a combine harvester

Opposition fans tend to keep up the agricultural theme against the Somerset team. Curiously, the same chants are also sung to fans of Bristol City and Rovers in England's sixth largest city.

I can't read

And I can't write

But that don't really matter

Cos I is a Yeovil Town fan

And I can drive my tractor

Steer to the left
Steer to the right
It don't really matter
Cos when it comes to shagging my wife
I'd rather 'ave me tractor.

You're going home on a combine harvester

General Chants

General Chants

We pay your benefits (over and over)

Sung by southern to northern clubs.

🎵: *'La Donna E Mobile'*

Is your tractor? (x2)
Is your tractor parked outside?

Sung to rural teams.

🎵: *'Bread Of Heaven'*

They're here, they're there
They're every f***ing where
Empty seats (x2)

Stands from Ikea
You bought your stands from Ikea

🎵: *'Guantanamera'*

I predict a diet

A chant for the more comfortable players.

𝄞: *Kaiser Chiefs' 'I Predict A Riot'*

You look in the dustbin for something to eat
You find a dead rat and think it's a treat
In your northern slums, in your northern slums!

You piss in the shower
You shit in the bath
You finger your gran and think it's a laugh
In your northern slums, in your northern slums!

Your dad's in the nick
Your mum's on the game
In your northern slums, in your northern slums!

You look at your dog in a frisky way
You give it a f**k and throw it away
In your northern slums, in your northern slums!

And a variation on the same family theme:

All you do is (x2)

All you do is f**k your mums!

: *'Bread Of Heaven'*

Me brother's in Borstal

Me sister's got pox

Me mother's a whore on the Liverpool Docks

Me uncle's a flasher

Me auntie's a slag

The Yorkshire Ripper's me dad!

Home to shag your sister

You're going home to shag your sister

: *'Guantanamera'*

Score in a brothel

You couldn't score in a brothel

&: *'Guantanamera'*

How high are your testicles? (over and over)

To teenage players.

𝄞: *'Go West'*

Get your tits out (x2)
Get your tits out for the lads

To fat players, cheerleaders and female match officials.

𝄞: *'Bread Of Heaven'*

You're Scouse
With a bit less class (over and over)

𝄞: *'Go West'*

You won the league, in black and white
You won the league in black and white
You won the league in the 50s
You won the league in black and white

𝄞: *'When The Saints Go Marching In'*

What's it like to? (x2)

What's it like to see a crowd?

To visiting fans from small clubs.

𝄞: *'Bread Of Heaven'*

We wish you a happy season (x3)

We won't see you next year

To teams facing the drop.

𝄞: *'We Wish You A Merry Christmas'*

Get your nostrils (x2)

Get your nostrils off the pitch

To managers with large noses.

𝄞: *'Bread Of Heaven'*

Chim chiminee, chim chiminee

Chim chim cheroo

How is life in League One treating you?

Works just as well with most relegated teams and divisions.

The wheels on your house
Go round and round
Round and round
All day long!

Bloggsy, wherever you may be
You are the king of child pornography
He goes in the showers with his little youth team
And while he's in there you should hear them scream

Supply name of choice.

𝄞: *'Lord Of The Dance'*

There's only one *Bryan Bloggs*
One *Bryan Bloggs*
With his packet of sweets
And his cheeky smile
Bloggsy is a f***ing paedophile

𝄞: *'Winter Wonderland'*

Who ate all the pies? (x2)

You fat bastard (x2)

You ate all the pies!

And the sausage rolls (x2)

You fat bastard (x2)

And the sausage rolls!

And the pasties too (x2)

You fat bastard (x2)

And the pasties too!

𝄞: *'Knees Up Mother Brown'*

You're shit and you're nearly Welsh (x2)

And ...

You're Welsh and you know you are (x2)

Both sung to border towns like Hereford, Chester and Shrewsbury.

𝄞: *'Go West'*

Keeper, keeper, where's your wife?

She's here

She's there

She's every-f***ing-where

She's a slag

She's a slag

Does she take it? (x2)

Does she take it up the arse?

A popular one for players with pretty celebrity wives.

🎼: *'Bread Of Heaven'*

Go to t'dole, cash giro

Go to t'pub, get plastered

Come home, beat up wife

Cos I'm a Northern bastard

A town full of inbreds

You're just a town full of inbreds

𝄞: *'Guantanamera'*

I've got a shed

It's bigger than this

I've got a shed that's bigger than this

It's got a door and a window

I've got a shed that's bigger than this

My rabbit hutch

Is bigger than this

My rabbit hutch is bigger than this

It's got a door and a rabbit

My rabbit hutch is bigger than this

Sung by visiting fans to small grounds.

𝄞: *'When The Saints Go Marching In'*

And in a similar vein, the old classic:

Shit ground no fans, shit ground no fans

Shit fans no songs, shit fans no songs

Shit fans no pride, shit fans no pride

𝄞: *'Big Ben Chimes'*

As for that useless ref:

All we want is a decent referee
A decent referee, a decent referee

𝄞: *'Yellow Submarine'*

The ref has got a tenner on the game (x2)
The ref has got a tenner (x2)
The ref has got a tenner on the game

𝄞: *'She'll Be Coming Round The Mountain'*

I'm blind
I'm deaf
I wanna be a ref!

The referee's
Got foot and mouth
The referee's
Got foot and mouth etc

The referee's
Got BSE
The referee's got BSE
He eats beef, beef and more beef
The referee's got BSE

𝄞: *'When The Saints Go Marching In'*

Are you Stevie? (x2)
Are you Stevie Wonder in disguise?

𝄞: *'Bread Of Heaven'*

Who's your father? (x2)

Who's your father, referee?

You ain't got one

You're a bastard

You're a bastard, referee

'Oh My Darling Clementine'

You're not fit to (x2)

You're not fit to ref non-league!

You're too fat (x2)

You're too fat to be a ref!

You're not fit to (x2)

You're not fit to wipe my arse!

'Bread Of Heaven'

We know where you live (x2)
You fat bastard (x2)
We know where you live!

𝄞: *'Knees Up Mother Brown'*

Sign on, sign on
With a pen
In your hand
You'll never work again
Sign on, sign on

Sung mainly at Everton and Liverpool fans.

𝄞: *'You'll Never Walk Alone'*

Often followed by:

You've got our stereos
TVs and videos

𝄞: *'La Donna E Mobile'*

They had to grease the turnstile just to get the bastard in (x3)
For he's a big fat bastard

Sung on sight of a fat spectator.

♪: *'Mine Eyes Have Seen The Glory'*

Bryan Bloggs is a virgin
He's never used his dick
He wanks in the shower
And sleeps in his own sick
He throws up to the left
He throws up to the right
And he couldn't pull a bird
If he tried all f***ing night

Supply your own name of player or manager.

♪: *'My Old Man's A Dustman'*

You've got the ugliest stewards in the land (x3)

♪: *'He's Got The Whole World In His Hands'*

The Bill!

It's just like watching *The Bill*

Sung when there is a large police presence at a match.

🎼: *'Blue Moon'*

Shit job, no friends

Shit job, no friends

Also to the police.

🎼: *'Big Ben Chimes'*

Who's that man with the helmet on?

Dixon, Dixon

Who's that man with the helmet on?

Dixon of Dock Green

On the beat all day, on the wife all night

Who's that man with the helmet on?

Dixon of Dock Green

I smell bacon
I smell pork
Run little piggy
I've got a fork

To the police.

Going down the motorway doing sixty-four
My gran let out a big one and blew me out the door
The engine couldn't take it
The car fell apart
Just because of my gran's supersonic fart
Fee Fi Fo Fum, I think I smell another one
Five-six-seven-eight, I think I'm gonna suffocate

One from more innocent times.

In church
It's just like being in church

One for especially quiet home supporters.

𝄞: *'Blue Moon'*

When I was just a little boy
I asked my mother – what will I be?
Will I be Chelsea? Will I be Spurs?
Here's what she said to me:
Wash your mouth out, son
Go get your father's gun
And shoot some Tottenham scum
It's the Reds for you

To the tune of 'Que Sera', a classic sung by most clubs, changing names of local rivals where appropriate. Likewise with another traditional terrace:

Tottenham Hotspur football club went to see the Pope (x3)
And this is what he said:
Who the f**k are Tottenham Hotspur? (x3)
The Reds go marching on, on, on!

Bryan Bloggs is illegitimate *(replace with name of least favourite player)*

He ain't got no birth certificate

He's got Aids and can't get rid of it

He's a *Belgian* bastard! *(replace with appropriate country/region)*

We'll be running round Wembley with our willies hanging out (x2)

We'll be running round Wembley, running round Wembley

Running round Wembley with our willies hanging out

Singing, I've got a bigger one than you (x2)

I've got a bigger, I've got a bigger, I've got a bigger one than you

 *'She'll Be Coming Round The Mountain'*

Back to school on Monday

You're back to school on Monday

Sung to baby-faced youngsters.

 *'Guantanamera'*

Sit down you t**t (x3)
Sit down
Sit down you t**t (x3)
Sit down

Sung at spectators arriving late, leaving early or handing out abuse.

♪: *'Auld Lang Syne'*

Cheerio, cheerio, cheerio (x3)
Cheerio, cheerio

Accompanied by a wave to a sent-off player or fans leaving early.

♪: *'Here We Go'*

You're dad is your mum's brother

♪: *'Go West'*

The following are all traditionally sung to the tune of 'Bread Of Heaven':

Does the Social? (x2)
Does the Social know you're here?

What's it like? (x2)
What's it like to be a t**t?

Shall we sing a (x2)
Shall we sing a song for you?

You're not fit (x2)
You're not fit to shag my mum

You're not famous (x2)
You're not famous any more

Sung to big clubs fallen on relatively hard times. In recent years this has been sung mainly at Liverpool, Leeds and Nottingham Forest.

Does your mother? (x2)
Does your mother know your dad?

Does your mother (x2)
Does your mother know you're here?

Does your mother (x2)

Does your mother know you're queer?

We can see you (x2)

We can see you sneaking out

International

International

England

Does your mummy? (x2)

Does your mummy know you're here?

England supporters voice concern for their Egyptian counterparts at Wembley.

♪: *'Bread Of Heaven'*

Just one Capello

Give him to me

Delicious manager, from Ital-eee!

Not heard a lot in the summer of 2010, however ...

You're not swimming any more!

England fans to USA fans at South Africa 2010, in the wake of the BP oil spill.

His name is Rio and he watches from the stand

He twisted his knee in a far and dusty land

England fans in South Africa after captain Ferdinand was injured in training.

♪: *Duran Duran's 'Rio'*

Crouch, Crouch, wherever you may be
You didn't stop at six-foot-three
You grew so tall
You're a legend on the ball
Now score us a goal at Wem-ber-lee

🎼: *'Lord Of The Dance'*

If it wasn't for the English you'd be Krauts (x2)
If it wasn't for the English
Wasn't for the English
If it wasn't for the English you'd be Krauts

Sung to the fans of any country that was occupied by the forces of Nazi Germany, but belted out with special feeling against the French, Belgians and Dutch.

🎼: *'She'll Be Coming Round The Mountain'*

Small town in Russia
You're just a small town in Russia

To Ukraine and other former Soviet states.

🎼: *'Guantanamera'*

Maradona is a wanker
He wears a wanker's hat
He's retired and fat now
But he's still a f***ing t**t
He f***ed up on the left wing
He f***ed up on the right
He had to cheat England
Cos the Argies are total shite

𝄞: *'My Old Man's A Dustman'*

You're shit
But your birds are fit

To Ukraine in Dnepropetrovsk.

𝄞: *'Go West'*

Ginger hair's a disability!

To Scots and Irish.

𝄞: *'You're So Shit It's Unbelievable'*

You mean f**k all to us (over and over)

Sung to Scots and Welsh.

𝄞: *'La Donna E Mobile'*

The shit part of England
You're just the shit part of England

Sung to Scots, Welsh, Northern Irish.

𝄞: *'Guantanamera'*

You can stick your f***ing Euro up your arse (x2)
You can stick your f***ing Euro
Stick your f***ing Euro
You can stick your f***ing Euro up your arse

Sung to anyone from the Eurozone silly enough to have abandoned their traditional currency.

𝄞: *'She'll Be Coming Round The Mountain'*

You'll never take the Falklands

Sung to Argentina. Repeat until a new war breaks out.

𝄞: *'The Referee's A Wanker'*

Are you Scotland? (x2)

Are you Scotland in disguise?

Sung to teams losing or playing poorly.

♪: *'Bread Of Heaven'*

Scotland

Is this the way to the San Siro?

I'm off the beer and on the vino

Scotland one, Italia zero

Oh Bonnie Scotland win for me

♪: *'Is This The Way To Amarillo?'*

Deep fry yer pizzas

We're gonna deep fry yer pizzas

Sung in Italy.

♪: *'Guantanamera'*

If you're Italian and you know it, shoot your fans

To the Italian police.

We hate England (x2)
We hate England more than you

To Welsh etc.
🎼: *'Bread Of Heaven'*

Save the snail (x2)
We're the famous Tartan Army and we're here to save the snail

Sung in Paris.

You can stick your Renault Clio up your arse (x2)
You can stick your Renault Clio
Stick your Renault Clio
Stick your Renault Clio up your arse!

To Thierry Henry.

You put your left hand in
Your left hand out
In out, in out
Then shake it all about
You do the Maradona and you turn around
He put the English out!

Oh Diego Maradona
Oh Diego Maradona
Oh Diego Maradona
He put the English out! Out! Out!

You put your right foot in
Your right foot out
In out, in out
Then shake it all about
You do the Chrissy Waddle and you turn around
He put the English out!

Oh Chrissy Chrissy Waddle
Oh Chrissy Chrissy Waddle
Oh Chrissy Chrissy Waddle
He put the English out! Out! Out!

You put your left foot in
Your left foot out
In out, in out
Then shake it all about
You do the Tommy Brolin and you turn around
He put the English out!

Oh Tommy Tommy Brolin
Oh Tommy Tommy Brolin
Oh Tommy Tommy Brolin
He put the English out! Out! Out!

You put your left foot in
Your left foot out
In out, in out
Then shake it all about
You do the David Batty and you turn around
He put the English out!

Oh David David Batty
Oh David David Batty
Oh David David Batty
He put the English out! Out! Out!

Hailing foreign goal-scoring heroes and English penalty-fluffers in the finals of major championships. Insufficient space here to include all verses.

♪: 'Hokey Cokey'

Sing karaoke
You only sing karaoke

Scotland fans to Japan supporters in Yokohama.

♪: 'Guantanamera'

S-C-O-T-S

We are S-C-O-T-S

We are S, super Scotland

We are C, completely barmy

We are O, on the bevvy

We are T, Tartan Army

Singing ... we are S-C-O-T-S

𝄞: *'D-I-S-C-O'*

Who put the ball in the England net?

Arfur, Arfur

Who put the ball in the England net?

Arfur, Arfur f***ing Europe

Who put the ball in the England net?

Olaf, Olaf

Who put the ball in the England net?

Olaf, Olaf f***ing Europe

This second verse only works if you have a) the thickest of Scottish accents or b) a throat full of rough oatcakes.

One team in Tallinn

There's only one team in Tallinn (x2)

Scotland fans try to see the funny side after the Estonia team failed to appear on the pitch for a World Cup qualifier, in a dispute over rescheduled kick-off time.

♪: *'Guantanamera'*

Wem-ber-lee! Wem-ber-lee!

Was the finest pitch in Europe

Till we took it all away

Wem-ber-lee! Wem-ber-lee!

We stole your goalposts

Your lovely goalposts

We stole your goalposts

And your Wembley pitch too

You never knew how much you'd miss them

Till we took your goalposts away

Scotland fans take a trip down memory lane to recall the day in 1977 when around 10,000 of their fathers stormed the pitch at Wembley for an unscheduled Bay City Roller look-alike competition.

♪: *'You Are My Sunshine'*

Sing when you're whaling

You only sing when you're whaling

Sung in matches against Norway and the Faroe Islands.

🎼 *'Guantanamera'*

Save the whales (x2)

We're the famous Tartan Army

And we're here to save the whales

🎼 *'Wem-ber-lee! Wem-ber-lee!'*

Wales

There's only one Johnny Hartson (x2)
He tips the scales and he plays for Wales
Walking in a Hartson wonderland

You can shove your Royal Family up your arse (x2)
You can shove your Royal Family
Shove your Royal Family
You can shove your Royal Family up your arse

You can stick your f***ing chariots up your arse (x2)
You can stick your f***ing chariots
Stick your f***ing chariots
You can stick your f***ing chariots up your arse

You can stick your Wayne Rooney up your arse (x2)
You can stick your Wayne Rooney
Stick your Wayne Rooney
You can stick your Wayne Rooney up your arse

♪: *'She'll Be Coming Round The Mountain'*

Mae hen wlad fy nhadau yn annwyl i mi
Gwlad beirdd a chantorion, enwogion o fri
Ei gwrol ryfelwyr gwladgarwyr tra mad
Dros ryddid collasant eu gwaed

Gwlad! gwlad! pleidiol wyf i'm gwlad
Tra môr yn fur
I'r bur hoff bau
O bydded i'r heniaith barhau

Hen Gymru fynyddig, paradwys y bardd
Pob dyffryn, pob clogwyn, i'm golwg sydd hardd
Trwy deimlad gwladgarol mor swynol yw si
Ei nentydd, afonydd i mi

Os treisiodd y gelyn fy ngwlad dan ei droed
Mae heniaith y Cymry mor fyw ag erioed
Ni luddiwyd yr awen gan erchyll law brad
Ni thelyn berseiniol fy ngwlad

Exactly so.

𝄞 'Land Of My Fathers', the Welsh national anthem.